T0328652

Cambridge Elements ≡

Elements in Anthropological Archaeology in the 21st Century
edited by
Eli Dollarhide
New York University Abu Dhabi
Michael Galaty
University of Michigan
Junko Habu
University of California, Berkeley
Patricia A. McAnany
University of North Carolina at Chapel Hill
John K. Millhauser
North Carolina State University
Rita Wright
New York University

FIRST CITIES

Planning Lessons for the 21st Century

Dean Saitta
University of Denver

CAMBRIDGE
UNIVERSITY PRESS

Shaftesbury Road, Cambridge CB2 8EA, United Kingdom

One Liberty Plaza, 20th Floor, New York, NY 10006, USA

477 Williamstown Road, Port Melbourne, VIC 3207, Australia

314–321, 3rd Floor, Plot 3, Splendor Forum, Jasola District Centre, New Delhi – 110025, India

103 Penang Road, #05–06/07, Visioncrest Commercial, Singapore 238467

Cambridge University Press is part of Cambridge University Press & Assessment, a department of the University of Cambridge.

We share the University's mission to contribute to society through the pursuit of education, learning and research at the highest international levels of excellence.

www.cambridge.org
Information on this title: www.cambridge.org/9781009475914

DOI: 10.1017/9781009338769

First published 2024

A catalogue record for this publication is available from the British Library.

ISBN 978-1-009-47591-4 Hardback
ISBN 978-1-009-33874-5 Paperback
ISSN 2753-6327 (online)
ISSN 2753-6319 (print)

First Cities

Planning Lessons for the 21st Century

Elements in Anthropological Archaeology in the 21st Century

DOI: 10.1017/9781009338769
First published online: March 2024

Dean Saitta
University of Denver
Author for correspondence: Dean Saitta, dsaitta@du.edu

Abstract: This Element describes and synthesizes archaeological knowledge of humankind's first cities for the purpose of strengthening a comparative understanding of urbanism across space and time. Case studies are drawn from ancient Mesopotamia, Europe, Asia, Africa, and the Americas. They cover more than 9,000 years of city building. Cases exemplify the 'deep history' of urbanism in the classic heartlands of civilization, as well as lesser-known urban phenomena in other areas and time periods. The Element discusses the relevance of this knowledge to a number of contemporary urban challenges around food security, service provision, housing, ethnic coexistence, governance, and sustainability. It seeks to enrich scholarly debates about the urban condition and inspire new ideas for urban policy, planning, and placemaking in the twenty-first century.

Keywords: ancient city, urban archaeology, urban history, comparative urbanism, history of city planning

ISBNs: 9781009475914 (HB), 9781009338745 (PB), 9781009338769 (OC)
ISSNs: 2753-6327 (online), 2753-6319 (print)

Contents

1 Introduction

Putting historical knowledge in the service of society has long been of interest to archaeologists. Fifty years ago, Richard Ford suggested that archaeological research can alert us to the catastrophic effects of land and resource mismanagement and offer guidance about how we can do better (Ford, 1973). In recent years, archaeologists have ramped up arguments establishing the relevance of archaeological knowledge to contemporary issues such as climate change, economic inequality, and social conflict (Sabloff, 2008; Ortman, 2019; Huvila et al., 2022).

Urban studies is just one of many interdisciplinary fields that can benefit from an infusion of archaeological knowledge. It is clear from the field's vast literature that we need more and better knowledge of cities in history in order to deal with contemporary questions and concerns. Scholars and practicing professionals – urban planners, designers, architects, and policymakers – are casting their net widely for new theories, models, and data sources that can inform contemporary practice. A special issue of the *Cambridge Journal of Regions, Economy and Society* covers some of this ground (Cox and Evenhuis, 2020). Suggestions for alternative paradigms of critical urban thought and practice are many and varied. They include planetary urbanization (Brenner, 2019), postcolonialism (Roy, 2009), pluriversal planning (Escobar, 2019, 2022a), and posthumanism (Houston et al., 2018; Jon, 2020). Interlocutors in these vigorous and enlightening debates urge us to learn from 'ordinary cities' of the Global South (Robinson, 2006) and geohistorical variations in urbanization processes (Fox and Goodfellow, 2022). Many argue that it is time to develop new 'normative visions' (Throgmorton, 2003) or 'imaginaries' (Taylor, 2019; Graeber and Wengrow, 2021; Zeiderman and Dawson, 2022) of what the city can be.

Urban sustainability – defined here as the persistence and resilience of cities through time – is an especially dynamic area of scholarship that is rich in opportunities for applying archaeological knowledge (Smith et al., 2021; Chase et al., 2023; Smith, 2023a). Advances in the development of geospatial methods such as LIDAR (light detection and ranging) reveal that urban or urban-like landscapes were much more extensive and durable in the human past than previously expected. Chronological issues in interpreting LIDAR and other geospatial data need working out, and scholars must always be mindful of the fact that ancient cities are palimpsests of multiple, intermixed processes. Nonetheless, current investigative methods have dramatically sharpened our picture of deep urban history. They have revealed an enormous diversity of urban forms and urbanizing processes and challenged us to develop theory for interpreting them. At the same time, archaeological knowledge relevant to contemporary urban studies has been rapidly accumulating in parts of the world that have never been on the radar of Western scholars, or where we never expected urban-like phenomena to exist. These areas include sub-Saharan Africa, North America prior to European conquest, and even the Amazon rainforest (Prümers et al., 2022; Walker, 2023).

The expanding geographical scope of archaeological studies combined with accumulating details about local expressions of urban life position us to better understand the material conditions, governance structures, and collective identities that allow cities to prosper and endure. The security, prosperity, livability, and sustainability of cities are matters of enormous global concern. In 2012, the World Urban Campaign declared that the battle for a sustainable future will be won or lost in cities. The United Nations' New Urban Agenda (United Nations 2017; Mehaffey and Haas, 2018) reaffirms the concern by urging that cities become more responsive to the needs of diverse individuals and groups; that is, we need to make them more inclusive, equitable, and just.

Accordingly, this Element has two overarching objectives. The first is to synthesize archaeological knowledge of ancient cities in a way that strengthens a comparative understanding of urbanism across time and space and, by extension, the field of urban studies. The second is to show how this body of knowledge is relevant to a number of challenges that concern urban scholars, planners, and policymakers today. These include challenges around food security, housing, service provision, ethnic coexistence, governance, and sustainability. The Element is animated by the conviction that there are useful lessons to be learned from the ancients in these areas. The hope is that this knowledge will enrich scholarly debates about the urban condition and generate new ideas for urban policy- and placemaking.

1.1 Defining the City

Defining the city has long perplexed archaeologists. My definition is a polythetic one that draws on a number of recent formulations (Hutson, 2016; Ortman, Lobo, and Smith, 2020; Pauketat, 2020a; Jennings et al. 2021; Smith, 2023a). The city is a more or less dense and permanent agglomeration of people in physical space that is characterized by diversity in cultural background and specialization of social roles. The essential centerpiece of city life is intense social interaction or 'energized crowding' (Kostof, 1991: 37) of the sort that generates innovation and affects a wider sustaining hinterland. This broad definition allows us to expand the sample of human settlements that can teach us about urbanizing processes.

By 'ancient' cities, I mean settlements that existed in the very deep past, at the origins of urbanity in the primary crucibles of civilization, such as

Mesopotamia, the Indus Valley, and Mesoamerica. My category of ancient also includes cities from the very recent past (as recent as 500 years ago) that, because of Western investigative biases (racial and other), have been neglected by scholars and thus might as well be ancient (e.g., precolonial sub-Saharan Africa, preconquest North America). The terms 'ancient' and 'first' are interchangeable in the context of this Element.

Finally, I define 'urbanism' as the theory and practice of city building that is cognizant of the social impact of the built environment – including the unbuilt spaces between buildings and other elements of the urban landscape – on the behavior and psychology of citizens. This definition subsumes the concept of 'urban design' and today's popular notion of urban 'placemaking'.

1.2 Organization

Section 2 provides historical background on how the ancient city has been studied from an archaeological perspective and describes two basic paradigms for investigating urban form and development. Sections 3 and 4 provide the case studies. They cover a huge swath of space (Figures 1, 2, and 3 map the

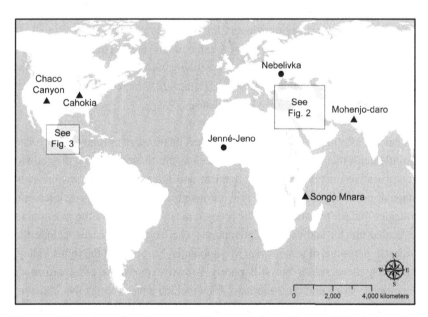

Figure 1 Location of settlements in Europe, Asia, Africa, and North America discussed in Sections 3 and 4. Circles indicate 'megasites' of questionable urban status. Triangles indicate cities with monumental architecture. The settlements cover the time period from 4000 BCE (Nebelivka) to 1500 CE (Songo Mnara). Map courtesy of John K. Millhauser.

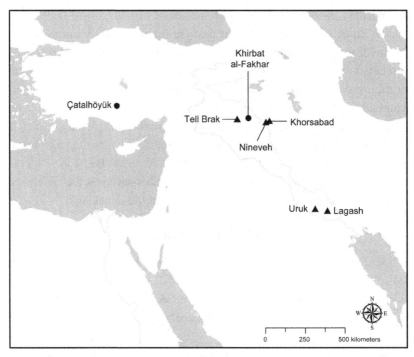

Figure 2 Location of settlements in Mesopotamia discussed in Section 3.
Circles indicate 'megasites' of questionable urban status. Triangles indicate
cities with monumental architecture. The settlements cover the time period from
7500 BCE (Çatalhöyük) to 681 BCE (Nineveh). Map courtesy of John
K. Millhauser.

settlements of primary interest) and more than 9,000 years of time (Table 1 lists
all settlements mentioned in the text). The cases are chosen for what they add to
a comparative understanding of urbanism and their potential to inspire new
imaginaries of city form. They provide insight into planning principles and
strategies that are translatable to the present, meaning they have the potential to
be 'scaled up' for addressing contemporary challenges. The cases include the
earliest expressions of urbanism in Mesopotamia, Europe, and the Indus Valley,
and much more recent but still poorly known expressions of urbanism in
precolonial Africa and the Americas. They include dense centers that conform
to typical expectations of what a city is, as well as low-density, dispersed, and
other 'anomalous' urban phenomena (Raja and Sindbæk, 2022).

    It is important to emphasize that the applied knowledge I seek in this study of
ancient urbanism does not depend on having a particular kind of relevant
historical analogue. It does not matter if the sample city is big or small,
centralized or dispersed, highly stratified or egalitarian. It does not matter if

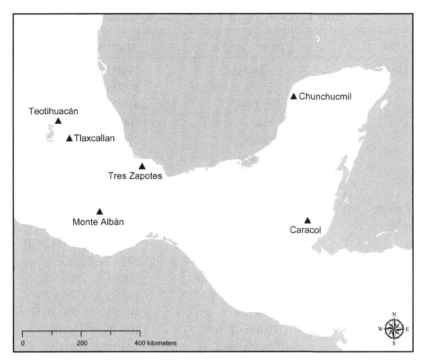

Figure 3 Location of settlements in Mesoamerica discussed in Section 4. The settlements cover the time period from 400 BCE (Tres Zapotes) to 1521 CE (Tlaxcallan). Map courtesy of John K. Millhauser.

the city is embedded in the world capitalist system or some other kind of world system (e.g., see Hall et al., 2011). It does not matter if the city was long- or short-lived. A short-lived but highly prosperous city in the ancient world can have something to teach about urban form and process that, in a different historical context or circumstance, might contribute to settlement durability and longevity. The search is for general principles and strategies of urban planning, placemaking, and governance that can be scaled up for modern contexts or that can be taken whole cloth as a guide to smaller-scale tactical interventions. Sections 5 and 6 discuss lessons learned for advancing comparative urban studies scholarship and for planning the twenty-first-century city. They establish a framework for how we should think about the urban past and present in order to maximize learning for a sustainable urban future.

2 Philosophical and Theoretical Orientation

This section provides background information relevant to the study. This includes a brief history of archaeological thought about cities in history and

Table 1 Archaeological sites mentioned in the text

Area	Sites	Approximate dates
Mesopotamia	Çatalhöyük	7500 BCE–6400 BCE
	Khirbat al-Fakhar	4400 BCE–3800 BCE
	Tell Brak	4200 BCE–3600 BCE
	Uruk	4000 BCE–3200 BCE
	Lagash	2900 BCE–2350 BCE
	Nimrud	822 BCE–723 BCE
	Khorsabad	717 BCE–706 BCE
	Nineveh	704 BCE–681 BCE
Europe	Nebelivka	4100 BCE–3600 BCE
Asia	Mohenjo-daro	2600 BCE–1900 BCE
	Harappa	2600 BCE–1900 BCE
Africa	Jenné-jeno	400 CE–800 CE
	Great Zimbabwe	1100 CE–1600 CE
	Songo Mnara	1355 CE–1500 CE
Mesoamerica	La Venta	1000 BCE–400 BCE
	Nixtun-Ch'ich	900 BCE–400 BCE
	Tres Zapotes	400 BCE–300 CE
	Monte Albán	500 BCE–800 CE
	Teotihuacan	100 BCE–600 CE
	Tikal	200 CE–900 CE
	Chunchucmil	400 CE–600 CE
	Caracol	600 CE–900 CE
	Tula	900 CE–1150 CE
	Mayapan	1150 CE–1450 CE
	Tenochtitlan	1325 CE–1521 CE
	Tlaxcallan	1300 CE–1521 CE
North America	Chaco Canyon	950 CE–1150 CE
	Cahokia	1050 CE–1250 CE

a summary of two basic philosophical orientations to the study of ancient cities that exist within the discipline: *scientific realism* and *interpretivism*.

2.1 Archaeologies of Urbanism

The first widely influential study of urbanism in archaeology was that of V. Gordon Childe (Childe, 1950). Childe offered an account of the 'urban revolution' by identifying ten abstract criteria that define the city and promoted a synthetic approach to understanding the city's origins. He saw the city as a dense, compact settlement supported by intensive agriculture that grew from the center out. Notable is the fact that Childe published this account in an urban studies journal, *Town Planning Review*. To that extent he was pioneering the kind of applied archaeology that is of growing interest today. However, Childe has also been criticized for holding a Eurocentric concept of the city that ruled out alternative urban forms (Chirikure, 2020).

One of the stronger intellectual heirs to Childe's legacy of theoretically informed, empirically based, and synthetic work is Michael E. Smith. Smith has been a leader for many years in subjecting ancient cities to systematic study, developing typologies for classifying and comparing them and demonstrating their potential to illuminate the role that cities play in contemporary life. These insights come together in his *Urban Life in the Distant Past: The Prehistory of Energized Crowding* (Smith, 2023a). Smith justifies the relevance of archaeological work by invoking a quote from Winston Churchill: "The farther backward you can look, the farther forward you can see." With numerous colleagues, Smith has produced a variety of empirical studies yielding insight into neighborhood organization, housing quality, residential segregation by class and ethnicity, access to urban services, wealth inequality, and use of open space (York et al., 2011; Smith et al., 2015; Dennehy et al., 2016; Stanley et al., 2016). The most important overall message of this work is its systematic and empirical substantiation of significant variation in every dimension of urban life analyzed. There is no 'typical' pattern that defines the city in any of the cultural traditions considered.

Monica L. Smith also has a long professional history investigating cities of the ancient world. She brings a vast amount of knowledge together in *Cities: The First 6,000 Years* (M. L. Smith, 2019). Like Michael E. Smith, Monica L. Smith seeks to put ancient and modern cities into comparative perspective; and, with other popularizers of urban history that invoke the ancient world (e.g., Kotkin, 2005; Clark, 2016; Rose, 2016), she emphasizes the contemporary city's roots in the distant past. Her concern is with the common patterns and continuities in transportation, sanitation, and resource provisioning that define the urban experience across time and space. Smith is optimistic about the urban future as long as three general findings about urban history are kept in mind: (1) infrastructure matters, especially where it serves the needs and interests of diverse cultural groups; (2) socioeconomic hierarchies are inevitable; and (3) consumption is ubiquitous – including the production of 'bling' to signal a variety of social statuses and identities.

In *Killing Civilization: A Reassessment of Early Urbanism and Its Consequences*, Justin Jennings (2016) offers a similarly sweeping view of ancient cities contextualized within a broader critique of the concept of 'civilization'. He challenges the popular notion that the bundle of characteristics traditionally used to define civilization evolved as a coherent package through a linear, step-like process that produces, in turn, the state, the city, social complexity, writing, high art, and class stratification. Jennings argues that this tidy reconstruction does not satisfactorily explain the variation in early urbanism that is coming to light. Instead, he argues for generating new theories about the origin of the state and the city that *unbundle* these characteristics and allow them to develop independently. This unbundling accommodates the possibility that the state and other forms of political complexity *follow* the city rather than precede it. In fact, the early city may have been associated with bottom-up, nonhierarchical, decentralized forms of political complexity that impeded the development of the state and class stratification. Jennings is thus concerned to expose the radical 'otherness' of the past and promote a view of ancient cities as 'experiments' that sometimes succeeded and sometimes failed.

Glenn Storey's (2020) *The Archaeology of Ancient Cities* offers a classification of ancient cities that sorts them into *micro-urban* (small area/high population density), *hyper-urban* (large area/high density), and *hypo-urban* (large area, low density) forms. He describes a number of examples of each, some of which are discussed in this Element. Uruk in Mesopotamia is micro-urban; Teotihuacan in the Valley of Mexico is hyper-urban; lowland Maya cities are hypo-urban. Storey expands the purview to Africa, where he describes Great Zimbabwe as hypo-urban. He considers the North American examples of Cahokia and Chaco Canyon (discussed in Section 4.5), putting them in a group of disputed cases of urbanization. Storey emphasizes the great variability of urbanizing processes in the past and highlights the agency involved, i.e., cities emerge from negotiations between different segments of society (2020: 37). His overall conclusion is consistent with what is now becoming common knowledge among scholars: city formation across time and space, from the ancient world to the modern "was messy, full of false starts, and an experiment in every location where it arose" (2020: 143).

Many other scholars have joined together to produce edited volumes about the early city. Recent collections include Creekmore and Fisher's (2014) *Making Ancient Cities: Space and Place in Early Urban Societies*, Yoffee's (2015) *Early Cities in Comparative Perspective, 4000 BCE–1200 CE*, Gyucha's (2019) *Coming Together: Comparative Approaches to Population Aggregation and Early Urbanization*, and Farhat's (2020) *Landscapes of Preindustrial Urbanism*. Yoffee's (2009) review of three earlier volumes (M. L. Smith, 2003a; Storey, 2006, Marcus and Sabloff, 2008) is striking in its two major recommendations that intersect with the concerns of this Element: First, the need for archaeologists to engage with modern urban theory. This includes theory that views the city as a complex 'assemblage' of human and nonhuman materials that have power and agency, with mutually effective relationships between them (for a discussion of assemblage theory in urban studies, see McFarlane, 2011). Second, the need for archaeologists to make cities more 'plausible', i.e., to give the citizens living in them some flesh and blood, some agency (see also Cowgill, 2004). This means explicating the tensions, struggles, successes, and 'everydayness' of urban life. Archaeology is nicely positioned to accomplish both (e.g., see the contributions to Alt and Pauketat, 2020).

2.2 Paradigms of Archaeological Inquiry Today

Michael E. Smith (2023a) sorts today's paradigms for investigating the ancient city into a *scientific realist* approach and an *interpretivist* approach. I discuss each in turn and end with a call for a paradigm of *engaged pluralism* that respects their essential complementarity.

2.2.1 Scientific Realism

Advocates for urban science seek to produce general knowledge of the city that can have transhistorical predictive value. The approach is comparative and nomothetic; the aspiration is to generate well-founded regularities or covering laws of urban development. This requires large datasets that can be subjected to quantitative analysis. The focus is on general problems that affect city-dwellers everywhere – e.g., energy and resource extraction and the organization of socioeconomic networks. The hope is that revelation of 'fundamental generative processes' of urban development will help guide contemporary urban planning and policy.

One line of analysis in urban science is settlement scaling theory. It is based on arguments from Santa Fe Institute (SFI) scholars including Luis Bettencourt and Geoffrey West (Bettencourt and West, 2010). These authors argue that all cities follow essentially the same rules of development as a function of how human social networks typically operate in space. Population size and density are key driving variables. Analogies from mammalian biology are used to argue that all cities are 85 percent alike in the way they look, work, and evolve as a function of size. Cities are scaled-up versions of each other in much the same way that "a whale is a blown-up elephant, which is a scaled-up giraffe, all the way down to a mouse and shrew" (G. West, quoted in A. West, 2011). Bettencourt and West argue that the key to understanding cities, and solving their contemporary problems, depends on understanding these universal properties and not the leftover 15 percent of contextual factors – local geography, history, culture – that make cities individually unique.

Ortman et al. (2015) use archaeological data from the Valley of Mexico, including the great ancient city of Teotihuacan, to illustrate the approach. Teotihuacan (comprehensively described by Cowgill, 2015, and discussed in greater detail in Section 4.2) is located about 40 kilometers northeast of Mexico City. It was occupied between 100 BCE and 600 CE. With increases in settlement size, Teotihuacan's public monuments got bigger and more voluminous, as did its residential dwellings. These trends are used as proxy variables for social productivity (i.e., gross domestic product) and personal productivity, respectively. As urban populations increase in size and density, per capita productivity and efficiency also increase. So too do disparities in household size and wealth as measured by the Gini coefficient, where a value of 1.0 indicates the highest level of inequality and a value of 0 indicates the lowest level (we will return to this measure of inequality in Section 4). Over time, the top 10 percent of Valley households came to encompass 40–50 percent of the total housing area. Thus, like modern cities the benefits of increasing urban size are neither widely nor equitably shared across the resident population. The city's status as a 'social reactor' is enhanced with scalar increases in size, but this comes at a social cost. Ortman and colleagues pitch their approach as a way to help cities maximize productivity and be more efficient in their development.

2.2.2 Interpretivism

An indisputable virtue of urban science in archaeology is that it makes the past relevant to the modern world. Urban science breaks down the opposition we tend to create between past and present. This approach to comparative urbanism encourages us to see ancient and modern cities within the same framework of reference. This is all to the good. However, a growing literature takes a critical look at urban science and highlights the limitations of a nomothetic, generalizing approach. In a review of Bettencourt's (2021) monograph on the subject, Goodspeed (2022) argues that urban science does not directly deal with the lived experience of city-dwellers. He argues that the complex social factors that shape urban form and life – the "plausibility" aspect highlighted by Yoffee – are not easily quantified. Dovey and Pafka (2016: 9) critique quantitative approaches more generally by noting that "the reduction of the city to its measurable components always comes at a cost, and central to what is lost are the lived intensities, rhythms, and socialities of everyday urban life." Similarly, Graeber and Wengrow (2021: 22) suggest that such reductionism can "impoverish history" and with it our "sense of possibility" of what an understanding of ancient cities can communicate. Hutson et al. (2023) demonstrate that scaling effects in cities depend on a variety of factors other than population, including the specifics of spatial layout and built form. In this respect, Batty (2022), in another review of Bettencourt's book, wonders what settlement scaling theory has to say about urban design, which so far is very little.

Generating the knowledge whose loss is lamented by the critics of urban science is the point of an alternative interpretive approach powered by *thick description*: the detailed explication of local context and relationships (Geertz, 1973) – or, if you will, a methodology of *storytelling*. The 15 percent of variation that is leftover in scientific studies of the city – the part that is about particularities and thus cannot be accounted for by general laws – is the stuff of storytelling. If we assume, following Kostof (1991), M. L. Smith (2019), and others (including Ortman, Smith et al., 2020) that the urban built environment is an active determinant of the *quality* of interactions that make cities the unparalleled social reactors that they are, then the particularities of ancient cities can serve modern urban planning and placemaking just as well as generalities. Grinsell (2020) puts the case well: although cities share in general processes of urbanization, what sticks with us are their idiosyncrasies, the things that cannot be abstracted. We need to be alert to the particularities of what makes cities unique in a specific place and time.

Interpretivist approaches focus on the particular ways in which ancient cities were irreducibly or qualitatively different from those in the modern world. They allow that detailed studies of the ancient city – properly translated and scaled up – can inform small-scale interventions for meeting urban challenges today. Smith (2023a: 27) suggests that interpretivist approaches are fundamentally anti-scientific if they embrace relativism or a radical skepticism that the past can be objectively known. However, storytelling about the past is no less realist than scaling studies, and interpretivists also embrace archaeology as an empirical, historical science. The difference is that stories have a way of resonating with people, of burrowing into their consciousness. Robust, place-based narratives anchored in specific settings defined by buildings, landscapes, and other spaces are compelling by producing a 'feel' for, or experience of, a place that quantitative studies cannot provide (Filep et al., 2014). The methodology is essential for making cities plausible in Yoffee's sense, i.e., for capturing urban lived experience and the human agency that shapes it.

Commitment to an interpretivist approach also supports the integration of Indigenous perspectives into archaeology and urban studies. This is a project of considerable importance if we are concerned to decolonize both fields, that is, to introduce ideas and understandings historically marginalized by Western science. Mathews (2022) calls for expanding the 'framing epistemology' of conservation studies to include Indigenous perspectives that view the world as a complex assemblage of land, water, climate, materials, and other life-forms (for a comparable perspective from the standpoint of archaeology, see Millhauser and Earle, 2022). The same argument has been made for urban studies (Houston et al., 2018). Even scholars committed to the development of urban science in archaeology see the incorporation of Indigenous and descendant voices as a priority (e.g., Smith et al., 2023). For Ortiz (2023), the challenge is not to stop telling stories but to decolonize storytelling, as authors like Jennings, Graeber, Wengrow, and others discussed in this Element attempt to do. We reject or underestimate the power of stories at our own peril. The challenge is to write them in ways that respect urban science and other accumulated knowledges (Izdebski, 2022).

2.3 Synthesis: An Engaged Pluralism

McMillan (2022: 929) notes that "making cities known comes with an epistemological challenge. No image of the city sees all, no text of the city expresses everything, no set of numbers holistically renders the world it contains." Years earlier, Tilly (1996: 704) noted that "cities offer privileged sites for study of the interaction between large social processes and routines of local life," implicating the need for studies of both the general and the particular. Chwalczyk (2020), commenting on SFI scaling research, insists that urban science must be supplemented with sociological and anthropological approaches of high resolution.

These critiques and arguments, taken together, suggest that we need a methodology that is something like the 'engaged pluralism' described by Barnes and Sheppard (2010). This epistemological orientation has two key features: (1) putting general and particular studies in conversation with each other and (2) using both of them to address societal needs (see also Box-Steffensmeier, 2022). Pluralistic approaches seek to 'weave' together Indigenous and non-Indigenous epistemologies to create new narratives of history and new visions for the future. Happily, there is a rich body of work about storytelling in urban planning that sees the enterprise as equal parts science and craft (Sandercock, 1998; Throgmorton, 2003; Hoch, 2022). Ortiz (2023) understands storytelling as the cornerstone of planning practice and as an indispensable skill for triggering change. This requires more inclusive and, indeed, 'insurgent' planning histories cognizant of the lived experiences of multiple communities.

Urban scientists themselves understand that realism and interpretivism are not irreconcilable. Bettencourt (2021: 381) acknowledges that the sciences and humanities must converge if the goal is to create processes of global development that are equitable and environmentally sustainable. Smith (2023a, 2023b) admits that interpretive understandings of the past provide useful data and findings that can guide the formulation of new research questions. Fulminante (2021) and Dufton (2022) assert that quantitative and qualitative studies of the ancient world can and should complement each other. Perhaps the most important observation is that of Michael E. Smith (2023a: 239), who notes that spatial analysis of early cities is a topic where "methodological advances are running far ahead of theory and comparative understanding." If that is true, then a historical science of ancient city life and development is best served by embracing a variety of philosophical approaches to knowing. There is surely room for the nomothetic and the idiographic, the plural and the particular (Schwenkel, 2022) to work together. All have a role to play in understanding the urban past and generating new visions for the urban future.

3 Development of First Cities in Mesopotamia, Europe, Asia, and Africa

In this section, I consider urban formations in two heartland areas of cultural development (Mesopotamia, the Indus Valley) and two 'outliers' (Europe and sub-Saharan Africa). Figures 1 and 2 map the settlements of primary interest.

3.1 Mesopotamia

Ancient Mesopotamia is generally regarded as the birthplace of cities. When and where this happened is a matter of some debate. Attention is usually focused on Çatalhöyük, a large, densely occupied (5,000–8,000 people) settlement in Turkey dating to 7500 BCE. Scholars have recognized neighborhood organization at Çatalhöyük and identified open spaces and alleys that may have served to differentiate neighborhoods (Hodder and Pels, 2010; Düring, 2013). The settlement's original excavator, James Mellaart (1967) originally pitched Çatalhöyük as the world's first city. Ian Hodder, who took over the excavations, categorizes it as a "very, very, very large town" (Hodder, 2006: 98). Storey (2020) views Çatalhöyük as a "stillborn" city, as does Jennings (2016). Michael E. Smith (2023a: 22–23) cannot see Çatalhöyük as fitting any definition of urban and proposes the label 'agrotown': a large nucleated village without urban functions and with a low level of social complexity. Taylor (2012) reasserted the site's urban status, an argument that was effectively countered by Smith et al. (2014). Der and Issavi (2017) see Çatalhöyük as a 'megasite' from which we can learn something about urbanism as a *process* if not a *product*. They argue that urbanism is best formulated as a flexible concept having a multiplicity of meanings and adaptable to a diversity of settlements and trajectories of growth and decline (see also Leadbetter, 2021; Sindbæk, 2022; Raja and Sindbæk, 2023; Smith, 2023a: 97).

Urban developments after Çatalhöyük are much less ambiguous and controversial. However, there is little widespread conformance with the model of city form and growth originally formulated by Childe. Instead, we see wide variation that suggests alternative approaches to placemaking and governance, as well as diverse causal processes.

Scholars now recognize that ground zero for urban origins was in northern Mesopotamia. Jason Ur (2020) summarizes what we know from two early settlements. Kirbat al-Fakhar in Syria dates from 4400 BCE to 3800 BCE. Ur sees it as a proto-urban megasite of 30,000 to 60,000 people covering an area about thirty times the size of Çatalhöyük (Ur, 2016: 141). Here, small villages or other communities came together without establishing a nucleated center. Spaces exist between village groupings in order to preserve social distance and thereby prevent conflict. The open space may have served as plots for cultivation. Kirbat al-Fakhar was an important site for the manufacturing and trade of obsidian tools and other commodities.

Tell Brak in Syria, dating 4200 BCE to 3600 BCE (McMahon, 2013a) is viewed by Ur as an example of a low-density city – the first recognized outside of the tropics (see Section 4). A low-density city is a settlement form in which agricultural and open land is interwoven with urban infrastructure and a dispersed residential population that is civically integrated (Lucero et al., 2015: 1140). As with Kirbat al-Fakhar, Tell Brak shows vacant space between settled areas. There is evidence for distinct ethnic enclaves and/or other kinds of social segmentation. However, tensions here could not be contained given evidence for significant violence at the settlement's founding (McMahon, 2014; Maaranen et al., 2022). Residents eventually learned to live with difference. Tell Brak grew inwardly in a manner that produced a dense nuclear core focused on a major temple. Whereas the rationale for Kirbat al-Fakhar may have been exclusively economic, Tell Brak became an ideological force that attracted immigrants and successfully integrated diversities. It also evolved, by 3800 BCE to 3600 BCE, a mixed-use edge zone with various industries, dumps, and burial grounds that bear resemblance to a modern city (McMahon, 2014).

Urban growth in Mesopotamia was generally organic for the first several millennia, as small settlements coalesced into larger entities containing streets, walls, and monumental architecture. After that, cities developed in fits and starts with occasional population declines and resurgences. Interestingly, Mesopotamian processes of urban growth seem to be governed by the normal mode of agricultural people provisioning households along kinship lines. Monica L. Smith (2003b: 21) notes that the average size of a residential neighborhood in early Mesopotamian cities (one hectare) approximates the size of a small agricultural village. This suggests the persistence in early cities of an organizing social structure predicated on face-to-face, kin-based relationships. Ur (2014: 264) argues that Mesopotamian cities acted like overgrown villages and notes that the Mesopotamians themselves used the same word to describe settlements of any size, scale, or internal structure (see also McMahon, 2013a: 33). Ur (2014: 262; 2016: 144) also notes the architectural similarity between buildings in these cities. What we see as temples and palaces were, to Mesopotamians, recognizable as traditional houses writ large. Thus, the city and its monuments originated as a metaphorical, 'scaled-up' version of kinship relations. Jason Jennings (2016) makes the interesting point that early cities in Mesopotamia were characterized by moral economies (M. L. Smith, 2019: 219 uses the phrase 'moral codes') that linked the city's prosperity with one's own.

Studies of later cities affirm that they were magnets for ethnic and cultural diversity (Emberling, 2015; Otto, 2015). Population sizes varied between 30,000 and 120,000 (Otto, 2015). Uruk (4000 BCE to 3200 BCE) was a city of 2.5 square kilometers that pulled up to 80 percent of the population out of the surrounding countryside, effectively ruralizing it. Thus, urbanization in Mesopotamia must have suggested to the participants the dawning of a new 'Urban Age'. Gwendolyn Leick (2001: 37) describes Uruk as containing well-planned public spaces and 'permeable' buildings that were designed for maximum accessibility, with care taken to ensure easy pedestrian circulation.

Lagash (2900 BCE to 2350 BCE) offers an interesting example of a 'heterogeneous' urban form (Hammer, 2022: 13). It was occupied during a time when southern Mesopotamia was at its most urbanized, with cities estimated to contain up to 90 percent of the population (McMahon et al., 2023). Lagash also challenges the traditional Childean model of urban growth from the center out. Scholars report a discontinuous, multicentric layout. A variable street pattern suggests diverse ethnic origins of the city's inhabitants (Hammer et al., 2022). The city incorporated water courses and marshlands along with agricultural areas. Empty, low-density space may have supported informal economies and perhaps housing. Neighborhoods appear to have been nonsegregated by status. Hammer (2022) describes Lagash as a type of 'marsh-based' urbanism and suggests that it may imply a different distribution of social power than traditional top-down models where power emanates from a central authority.

Assyrian cities in the second and first millennia BCE display more concerted investments in formal, centralized urban planning, including the construction of walls, gates, processional ways, and well-ordered ceremonial precincts. However, these cities still exhibit lots of variation and hybrid combinations of planned and unplanned areas. The existence of informality does not mean that central planning was absent. Adam Smith (2003: 225–226) puts it well: too strict of an adherence to the 'organic' versus 'planned' binary risks mistaking cultural variation in aesthetics (born of history and context) for decentralized urban planning. Juxtaposed houses of different sizes suggest social mixing. However, Keith (2003) urges caution: smaller houses could be the in-town apartments of elites who had larger villas outside the city. The diversity of these cities invites theory about what motivated their design and how people lived in them (Otto, 2015).

The sequence of cities in Assyria illustrates several important points about urban form and function. Studies of ancient Nimrud (822 BCE to 723 BCE) suggest that there was lots of latitude for citizens to create and evolve their cities (Ur, 2013). Informal housing was a ubiquitous feature of Mesopotamian cities. It may have even put pressure on imperial planners to make temporary interventions permanent with walls, pavements, cul-de-sacs, and other material features (Creekmore, 2014). This is the great hope of 'tactical urbanists' today: that city planners will embrace and formalize planning innovations produced by engaged citizens at the local, neighborhood level.

Later designed Mesopotamian capitals display some audacious exercises in city building that provide insight into unusual planning principles. Khorsabad (Dur-Sharrukin) is one of them. Between 717 BCE and 706 BCE, King Sargon II constructed his visually prominent citadels directly astride the city walls. In so doing, Sargon worked the edge rather than the center, thereby increasing the visibility of his monuments to a broader cross-section of society. This was clearly an exercise in projecting political power. However, from the inside the palace had a certain openness and permeability (Novak, 2004; McMahon, 2013b). Here, Sargon eschewed architectural symmetries – and the visual images of order and power that they communicate – in favor of asymmetries. The resulting complex plays of light and shadow produced desired sensory effects on visitors as they moved through buildings and courtyard spaces (McMahon, 2013b). Indeed, by channeling movement between spaces that are alternately light and dark the palace at Khorsabad is an excellent example of architecture serving to produce 'enticement' and 'mystery'. Cognitive scientists have argued that these physical properties have an evolutionary benefit for humans by encouraging exploration of novel environments (for a review of studies, see Hildebrand, 1999). Goldhagen (2017) discusses the resonance for the human mind of patterned complexity and narrative in architecture of the sort that is evident at Khorsabad. Thus, there is important planning and design knowledge embedded in the architectural form and configuration of ancient monuments that is worth retrieving if we want to create buildings today that draw people in and reaffirm a shared cultural identity (see also Thomason, 2016; Van De Mieroop, 2003).

Mesopotamia's most compelling example of central planning and urban experimentation is arguably Nineveh in the reign of Sennacherib, 704 BCE to 681 BCE. The city's resident population numbered up to 75,000 people (Otto, 2015). Leick (2001: 231) suggests that Sennacherib's "restless experimentation" with innovative technical solutions to urban problems and his use of "flexible strategies" in urban design make him an unusual Assyrian ruler and, for sure, a pioneering urbanist. At the time a small and run-down city, Sennacherib undertook in Nineveh a program of historic preservation, restoring dilapidated temples to previous glory. He also widened Nineveh's public squares and straightened its streets to bring in more sunlight. However, Sennacherib writes: "If ever (anyone of) the people who dwell in that city tears down his old house and builds a new one, and the foundations of his house encroach upon the royal road, they shall impale him upon a stake on his own house" (Van De Mieroop, 1997: 78–79). Otto (2015) suggests this passage indicates that the city administration had ultimate responsibility for real estate development and that there were limits to the exercise of individual agency.

In sum, Mesopotamian cities were variable and diverse right from their humble beginnings as scaled-up versions of early farming villages. Emberling (2015) notes that our picture of the Mesopotamian city is, as a consequence of deficiencies and gaps in archaeological data, a 'pastiche' stitched together from different cities and different time periods, and that it is a largely static model that misses variation and nuance (see also Baker, 2023). In reality, Mesopotamian cities were interesting hybrids of planned (e.g., city cores) and unplanned (e.g., neighborhood) spaces. They embodied narratives about cosmology and imperial power. Architects used complex assemblages of buildings and spaces to provide dramatic sensorial experiences. Other aspects of Mesopotamian cities are unclear, including the functional nature of open spaces. We lack knowledge about urban edge zones and transitions between urban and nonurban spaces (McMahon, 2013a). We also lack physical evidence of markets. McMahon (2013a) suggests that edge zones may have been the locus of vibrant commercial exchange, as well as intercultural interaction. In any case, the traditional Childean model of what early cities were like and how they evolved is not entirely accurate and may never have been accurate (Leyser et al., 2018; Hammer, 2022).

3.2 Europe: The Case of Trypillian Megasites

Developing concurrently with the earliest Mesopotamian low-density megasites were similarly novel and enigmatic settlements in the Cucuteni-Trypillia culture area encompassed by the modern countries of Romania, Moldova, and

Ukraine. These settlements (conservatively dated from 4100 BCE to 3600 BCE) go by various names: agglomeration sites, 'anomalous giants', and low-density cities. Scholars propose a number of models ranging from large, permanent full-time settlements to small, seasonally enlarged settlements. An accumulating literature (Gaydarska, 2016, 2021; Müller et al., 2016; Chapman, 2017; Diachenko and Menotti, 2017; Chapman et al., 2019; Gaydarska et al., 2023) describes these settlement phenomena, debates their meaning, and ponders their implications for understanding variation in early urbanism.

Trypillian settlements were highly structured using some combination of four basic planning principles: (1) a circular, concentric arrangement of structures, (2) internal radial streets, (3) sectoral growth in quarters, and (4) a vast inner open space. Central open spaces were likely dedicated to multiple functions: corralling of animals, specialized pottery production, flintknapping, craft fairs, games, feasts, and other ceremonies and rituals (Gaydarska and Chapman, 2022: 19–20). All four planning principles are evident at Nebelivka, one of the largest of the Trypillian settlements. Nebelivka covered 238 hectares, which is comparable to Uruk at its peak. It contained 1,500 structures, 14 residential quarters, and 160 neighborhoods. Its central open area covered 65 hectares. Public architecture included twenty-three mega-structures interpreted as assembly houses. These appear to be regularly distributed across a settlement populated by up to 46,000 people coming from up to 100 kilometers away.

Intriguingly, in their spatial layout Trypillian megasites bear formal similarity to Black Rock City (aka 'Burning Man'), a contemporary utopian gathering held every year in the Nevada desert that attracts visitors from all over the world (Figure 4). Its occupation ends with the burning of a large man-like structure at the camp's open center. Burning Man's large size and other city-like qualities have attracted the attention of contemporary urban planners (Berg, 2011) and even Nobel Prize laureates (Badger, 2019).

Investigators of Trypillian megasites suggest that residents made determined efforts to integrate multiple local identities and cultivate a common identity using painted ceramics, figurines, and other material cultures (Chapman et al., 2019). Gaydarska (2021) sees governance as being collectively distributed across groups. Settlement organization appears to embody principles of social inclusion and self-expression, gift/barter economies, and civic responsibility – an ethos that has been explicitly articulated for Burning Man. There is even evidence that the settlements were purposely burned at their abandonment and then rebuilt later, a discovery that gives the comparison to Burning Man some added resonance. There is debate about why the megasites disappeared around 3600 BCE. Gaydarska (2019) suggests that this was not about the introduction of new

Figure 4 Black Rock City (aka Burning Man) aerial view. Photograph by Kyle Harmon, distributed under Creative Commons Attribution-2 Generic license.

Source: Wikimedia Commons, https://commons.wikimedia.org/wiki/File: Burning_Man_aerial_view.jpg.

technologies or environmental change but rather about emerging challenges to the traditional use of space, the power of household groups, and the governing communitarian ideology. Hofmann et al. (2019) suggest a process of social fissioning as emerging hierarchical decision-making models were rejected by communities politically organized into autonomous segmented lineages.

Scholars not directly involved in the archaeological work raise serious questions about the urban status of Trypillian settlements. Smith (2023a: 52) does not consider them urban because they lack social heterogeneity and urban functions. However, he also suggests that they can still yield "useful insights" for the analysis of urbanism. Likewise, Harding (2018) considers it inappropriate to see them as urban in character but realizes that they are a step in that direction. Ohlrau (2022) rejects Trypillian settlements as low-density cities but still considers them important for theorizing early urbanization as a *process*. Graeber and Wengrow (2021: 297) take the most prudent, albeit provisional position: they are reminders of the "proof that highly egalitarian organization has been possible on an urban scale." They may contain insights for planning low-density cities today, implementing participatory design, and fostering a collective culture of citizenship.

3.3 Asia: The Indus Valley

Another original cradle of civilization is the Indus Valley of Pakistan and Western India. Developments here are comprehensively described and analyzed by Rita Wright (2010). The Indus exhibited two cycles of urbanization (Petrie, 2013). I focus on the earliest, from 2600 BCE to 1900 BCE. Five unusually large settlements from this time period have been investigated, the most famous being Mohenjo-daro and Harappa. Although there are some variations in planning and architecture (Lawler, 2008; Petrie, 2013), the original Indus cities have broadly comparable overall layouts. They have a consistent order as evidenced by semi-orthogonal gridding, paved streets, and formal gateways into the city. An irregular, organic pattern of streets and passageways is also evident. Thus, there are questions about the extent to which their planning was centralized. They were certainly cosmopolitan and global, as indicated by the evidence for trade with Mesopotamian cities (Clark, 2016: 35). Petrie (2019: 127) suggests that Indus cities, like those in Mesopotamia, are scaled-up versions of earlier agricultural settlements, with monumental public architecture emulating the form of earlier houses. It is interesting that Indus cities contain small blocks and abundant intersections. Because of the options this configuration provides for navigating the city – including escaping potentially uncomfortable encounters with strangers – Indus cities fit securely into the cognitive and evolutionary scientist's ideal form of a city (e.g., Sussman and Hollander, 2015: 31).

Indus cities were culturally and ethnically diverse. This is evidenced by the biological variation among individuals buried in city cemeteries (Kenoyer et al., 2013; Valentine et al., 2015; Robbins Schug, 2020) and local variation in craft production techniques (Smith, 2006). Immigration into the cities from the sustaining hinterland may have been substantial, especially during the market season. Kenoyer (2003) suggests that the population for Harappa may have swelled to 80,000 at that time. Widely shared similarities in material culture production and use – black painted/red-slipped pottery, carved steatite bowls, cubical weights, ceramic figurines, shell bangles and beads, and copper tablets (which may have functioned as coinage; see Kenoyer, 2003) – bound the cities and their sustaining hinterlands together. This shared set of artifact styles and religious symbols has been interpreted as a 'veneer' on top of local patterns of considerable diversity (Davis, 2017; Petrie et al., 2017). Thus, it may have constituted a unifying ideology or civic 'brand' that served the cause of social cohesion.

Mohenjo-daro in Pakistan is especially interesting. The 2.5-kilometer-square city contained a population of 40,000 (Yoffee, 2005). It is spatially divided into a 'citadel' (an acropolis of fired brick) and a 'lower town' of modular residential architecture, separated by open space. The citadel appears to be nonresidential, limited to public building including a spacious 'pillared hall' that could have accommodated hundreds of people (Green, 2022). Archaeologists are not sure how to interpret the open space (Green, 2022). Possibilities that come to mind include additional public space, an agricultural commons, or an area for informal housing.

Mosher (2017) provides some insight into the structure of Mohenjo-daro's neighborhoods. He identifies multiple walled sectors and centers (see also Wright, 2010; Green, 2021). However, it is interesting that neighborhood boundaries are difficult to locate. The implication is that internal walls functioned as permeable edges rather than hard and fast boundaries. There is no evidence that neighborhoods were ethnically segregated. There seems to be inequality in house sizes and certain artifact hoards containing exotic materials are differentially distributed, but otherwise wealth differentiation appears limited. Streets and thoroughfares were respected as public goods into which houses could not protrude (Green, 2022).

Also functioning as public goods were the impressive and complex water management facilities in Indus cities. Nearly all houses contained bathing facilities. Streets incorporated numerous wells, pipes, gutters, and drains. The latter moved waste out of the city via brick-lined channels. Water management also figured in the architecture of social and religious integration. Mohenjo-daro's central citadel featured a 'Great Bath' as a distinctive piece of monumental architecture. It may have played a role in public cleansing rituals. Monica L. Smith (2006) suggests that the health of citizens across the Indus was generally pretty good. Certainly, Mohenjo-daro's system of water management is as historically significant as the nineteenth-century infrastructural innovations and improvements made in Paris under Baron Georges-Eugène Haussmann or in London under Joseph Bazalgette. Thus, it is reasonable to see Mohenjo-daro as our earliest example of the 'eco-city'.

Where civic administration is concerned, Mohenjo-daro yields no images of individual rulers, no burials of kings or queens, and no evidence of a ruler cult (Blanton and Fargher, 2008: 62; B. Chase et al., 2014; Yoffee, 2016; Green, 2021). The evidence for palaces is ambiguous. Vidale (2010) suggests that larger houses might be the residences of elites because some of them have a physical form that mirrors that of the Great Bath. Green (2018) has identified distinctive small structures located near public spaces and street intersections. These buildings had thick walls and multiple entrances. They were 'permeable' and became more so over time. These structures may have served as places where distinct social groups negotiated their differences (see also Petrie, 2019). They may be ancient analogues for what contemporary urbanists describe as public 'third spaces': Amin's (2006: 1020) "prosaic spaces of civic inculcation," Wood and Landry's (2008: 260) "spaces of day to day exchange," or Anderson's (2011) "cosmopolitan canopies." If there were palaces at Mohenjo-daro, they may not have been for the elite, but rather they may have been intended as "palaces for the people" (Klinenberg, 2018).

The positive evidence in the Indus for well-provisioned cities offering extensive and equitable access to life-sustaining resources, public amenities, and consumer goods suggests the early manifestation of a sharing economy that served an ethos of 'just sustainability' (Agyeman, 2013; McLaren and Agyeman, 2015: 88–89). The absence of evidence for hierarchical rulership suggests collective governance combining *some* form of centralized authority with strong citizen autonomy at the local level. In other words, a system of 'heterarchical' power-sharing and decision-making among corporate groups, neighborhood associations, or guild-like organizations around craft industries. Carole Crumley offers the authoritative definition of heterarchy in archaeology:

> Heterarchy may be defined as the relation of elements to one another when they are unranked or when they possess the potential for being ranked in a number of different ways. For example, power can be counterpoised rather than ranked. Thus, three cities might be the same size but draw their importance from different realms: one hosts a military base, one is a manufacturing center, and the third is home to a great university. (Crumley, 1995: 3)

Jonathan Mark Kenoyer (quoted in Lawler, 2008) suggests a model for Indus cities of polycentric power among competing elites who negotiated across a wide landscape. It is not clear that Indus cities were divided by function or role in the way that Crumley describes in her hypothetical example. However, the whole appears to have been bound together by a deeply rooted shared civic culture or identity as evidenced by the veneer of shared artifact styles and religious symbols. This dovetails with inferences that public architecture facilitated "mass deliberation and implementation" (Green, 2022: 14).

Although there are still many unanswered questions, Ben Wilson's (2020: 46) comment about Indus urbanism in his book *Metropolis* provides an appropriate coda. Wilson suggests that "Harappan [Indus Valley] urbanization holds out a promise: if you can get design right from the very beginning, your city becomes a place that draws out the best in humanity and lets its people flourish. The people of the Indus Valley seemingly cracked that conundrum."

3.4 Sub-Saharan Africa

Scholarly and popular interest in ancient African urbanism has long been focused on Egypt. One early view suggested that, because of the absence of good settlement evidence, Egypt was a 'civilization without cities' (Wilson, 1960).

This view is now rejected, and the debate about Egyptian urbanism is more nuanced (Bard, 2008). Michael E. Smith et al. (2015, see also Smith, 2023a:127–128) bring Egyptian cities fully within the scope of a comparative urbanism by noting similarities between worker compounds at the imperial capital of Amarna and company towns in the USA and Latin America.

Africa south of the Sahara, on the other hand, has always been a blind spot in global histories of urbanism. This long history of neglect is related to the 'colonial imagination' that saw Africa as essentially rural in character, consisting of undifferentiated villages of mud and thatch huts (McIntosh and McIntosh, 2003). If sub-Saharan Africa was urban at all, the condition was imposed from without, e.g., via contacts with the urban Islamic world. Alternatively, it is now empirically verified that sub-Saharan urbanisms are indigenous and widely variable in nature (Steyn, 2007; Asomani-Boateng, 2011; Chirikure, 2020). They not only were uniquely indigenous in nature but were influential in shaping broader Saharan, Atlantic African, and Indian Ocean patterns of life (Stahl, 2020: 43).

3.4.1 West Africa

The West African (Mali) city of Jenné-jeno, dating from 400 CE to 800 CE, is instructive as an early example of an ecologically and socially conscious low-density urbanism. The essential source is work by Roderick and Susan McIntosh (McIntosh, 1997; McIntosh and McIntosh, 2003; McIntosh, 2005). The Jenné-jeno urban complex consists of several clustered mound-based communities distributed within a 4-kilometer radius along the margins of the Niger River. Its population totaled up to 40,000 people. The mound centers appear to have been ethnically distinct but functionally interdependent, guided by principles of specialized craft production and the reciprocal exchange of goods and services within a generalized economy. This made good ecological sense in a dynamic and unpredictable environment characterized by high inter-annual variability in subsistence production.

Unlike ancient Egypt, however, Jenné-jeno was not stratified politically. Evidence for a dominant ruling class has never been found. McIntosh and McIntosh (2003) suggest that power was shared horizontally between corporate groups; that is, the governance was heterarchical. Monica L. Smith (2006: 116) sees clear similarities between Jenné-jeno and Indus cities in this regard. It is intriguing that, although separated by 2,500 to 3,000 years, Indus and West African cities implemented some of the same integrating or unifying principles while creating very different kinds of urban settlement: concentrated settlement in the Indus, clustered settlement along the Niger. Both developed overlapping domains of authority and unifying civic ideologies reflected by distinctive material assemblages.

It is unlikely that Jenné-jeno's unique 'clustered cities' model of urban settlement can be transferred wholesale to today. But the case study has some relevance for imagining how eco-social interdependence among heterogeneous groups and its accompanying unifying ideology can be produced within contemporary cities. Indeed, we might be seeing some reflections of this ethos in the self-organizing qualities of the bottom-up, informal urbanism that characterizes the favelas and barrios of today's mega-cities in the Global South (McGuirk, 2014).

3.4.2 East Africa

The Swahili Coast is a second case study from sub-Saharan Africa that has more direct contemporary relevance. Urbanization occurred here between 500 CE and 1500 CE. The form was very different from that of Jenné-jeno. Walled 'stonetowns' were constructed out of rough coral and mortar. Evidence suggests that the stonetowns are an indigenous urban form, not imposed by contact with the Islamic world as previously thought (Patel, 2014). However, the stonetowns were clearly embedded in global networks. They were outward-facing, oriented to economic opportunities provided by international trade. Like Mesopotamia and the Indus, East African cities drew people from afar afield: the immediate hinterlands as well as India and the Far East. Political leaders attracted followers by appealing to traditional forms of ancestor veneration (Robertshaw, 2019). This produced multiethnic, cosmopolitan cities. Wynne-Jones (2018) categorizes coastal settlements as 'emporia': places where a mixed population came together. Bissell (2018: 599) describes them as centers of "extraversion, creative incorporation, and flexible adaptation." Kusimba (2008) notes that town–hinterland relationships before 1500 CE were inclusive and noncoercive. This would change after 1500 with the onset of the global slave trade.

The stonetown of Songo Mnara provides an especially good window into the social and material dynamics of Swahili cities. Songo Mnara is located in southern Tanzania and was occupied from 1355 CE to 1500 CE (Fleisher, 2010). Its relatively short occupation and quick abandonment provides high data resolution (Wynne-Jones and Fleisher, 2015) and excellent insight into how citizens lived in the city. The city features a couple dozen housing blocks loosely arranged around three large open spaces with an enclosing wall. There are six mosques, four cemeteries, and elevated palace complexes in the southwest and northeast sections of the city. Economic production 'territories' crosscut social divisions (Wynne-Jones and Fleisher 2016). The enclosing city wall did not define the living or working areas of urban residents (Pawlowicz et al., 2021). Walls were constructed less for protection than for symbolic purposes. They marked the city as 'cultured space', inviting interaction from afar (LaViolette and Fleisher, 2004: 340). They also signaled, to foreign traders and investors, political stability and credit-worthiness (Bissell, 2018: 591). In other words, walls were part of the performance of cosmopolitanism (LaViolette, 2008). So too were the causeways that connected the city to the coast. Indeed, the entire material assemblage represents a monumental architecture of cosmopolitanism (Pollard et al., 2012).

Of particular interest are the open spaces in Swahili cities, such as those described at Songo Mnara (Figure 5) by Jeffrey Fleisher (2014). These areas defy classification according to the Western binary of public versus private space. Instead, they are versatile, multifunctional, and inclusive. They hosted public ceremonies and performances. But they also allowed room for urban gardens, trade kiosks, and workshops (shell and stone bead making, iron-smithing). Perhaps most strikingly, they accommodated informal housing. At Songo Mnara wattle-and-daub houses existed alongside public amenities and performance spaces. In many cases, houses were nestled up against city walls (Fleisher and Wynne-Jones, 2012), indicating that walls in Swahililand were both resistant *and* porous, much like those in the Indus. The informal housing would have been in full view of elites in their elevated palaces. Jervis et al. (2021) note that trade occurred within houses as well as in open space, lending support to Baumanova's (2022) observation that Swahili public and residential space was "entangled and interlinked." These observations call into question the ability of Swahili elites to exert full control over public space and suggest that the wider public shared in, and negotiated, civic power (Baumanova, 2020: 42). Thus, Songo Mnara seems a good example of how a city's public spaces can be dedicated to "mixed public use, without excessive surveillance, gating, privatization, or humiliation of minorities" (Amin, 2006: 1017). Jervis et al. (2021: 233) see a different form of surveillance in play, one that they describe as a form of 'communal guardianship' rather than an explicit imposition of control.

Other facts support the existence in Swahililand of a unique sort of open urbanism or 'urbanism for all'. The wattle-and-daub housing form was not limited to non-elites (Rødland et al., 2020; LaViolette et al., 2023). Elites also lived in earthen houses, so the binary of stone = elite housing and wattle-and-daub = commoner housing does not hold here as it typically does in other places (Pawlowicz et al., 2021). The occupants of earthen houses appear to have had roughly equivalent access to the same kinds of goods as those in the stone elite houses, including coins and expensive imported pottery (Patel, 2014).

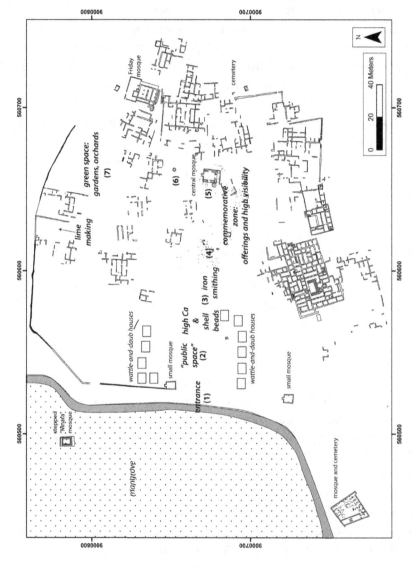

Figure 5 Songo Mnara site plan. Numbers indicate features and uses of public space (4 and 5 are graves and tombs; 6 is a well area). Location and number of wattle-and-daub houses are estimates. From Fleisher (2014), with permission of the author.

Thus, paralleling equitable access to space is a rough economic equality, at least in some dimensions.

Many years ago, Richard Hull (1976: 127) suggested that African cities "were at once utilitarian, ornamental, and humane." For Hull, urban living in Africa "radiated a spirit of mutual aid and cooperation, of civility and gentility." Songo Mnara's built environment, in particular, suggests that the city literally possessed what Richard Sennett (2013: 394–395) describes as the power of *teatro mundi* – theater of the world – a quality that separates active and vivacious public spaces from those that are monofunctional, well-ordered, and devoid of life. Although contrasting in settlement form and governance structure, with clustered/heterarchical at one end and more centralized/hierarchical at the other, Jenné-jeno and Songo Mnara are potentially rich in insights about how to create urban forms predicated on inclusion rather than exclusion (Fleisher, 2010). In Jenné-jeno's case, the forms were put in the service of Agyeman's just sustainability; in Songo's, to the creation of a genuinely cosmopolitan attitude. All of this reinforces Myers' (2011) point that ancient Africa is perfectly suited to contribute to ongoing debates about the urban condition. The continent is, in Stahl's (2020: 43) view, well-positioned to expand our horizons of what is possible in contemporary urban planning and placemaking.

4 Expressions of Ancient Urbanism in Mesoamerica and North America

Cities developed in many areas of the Americas well before the time of the European invasion. The earliest settlement to qualify as urban is likely Caral in north-central Peru. This monumental complex of pyramids, plazas, and residential buildings dates to the third millennium BCE (Solis, 2006). However, like Africa the Americas are not given sufficient attention as wellsprings of interesting and comparative urbanism. For example, the 900-page *Oxford Handbook of Cities in World History* (Clark, 2013) ignores the preinvasion Americas with the exception of passing reference in one chapter (Fernandez-Armesto, 2013). The record is becoming clear that Indigenous urbanisms in the Americas – from North to South – were substantial enough in their material form, geographical extent, and cultural impact to warrant chapter-length treatment in any comprehensive compendium of cities in world history (if we understand 'history' to include the entire time period of human existence on the planet and not just time periods for which we have written records). As with other regions of the world, we see physical and implied political variation right at the origins of urbanization. Figures 1 and 3 map the settlements of primary interest.

4.1 Urban Origins in Mesoamerica

The earliest expression of urban society in Mesoamerica is among Olmec peoples in the Veracruz and Tabasco areas of Mexico around 1200 BCE (Pool and Laughlin, 2022). The major Olmec settlement of La Venta (1000 BCE to 400 BCE) establishes the fundamental, time-honored Mesoamerican urban configuration of a planned, central ceremonial core containing monumental buildings aligned to the cardinal directions, with houses of subjects scattered in the jungle beyond (Smith, 2017). The impression is one of hierarchical, autocratic governance (Feinman and Carballo, 2018).

But this appears to be just one of a number of early arrangements. The existence of an urbanism predicated on equity and collectivity is implicated by findings at the city of Tres Zapotes (Pool and Loughlin, 2016, 2017). Tres Zapotes started as a minor, outlying center in La Venta's sphere of influence. Around 400 BCE it came into its own as a political force after La Venta's influence waned. The city's primary investigator, Christopher Pool, suggests that the city was built on mass migration of presumably ethnically distinct people from La Venta and elsewhere (cited in Wade, 2017a). However, the city is distinctively different in both physical form and implied governance structure compared to La Venta. Monumental architecture is distributed in four separate plazas as opposed to one single large plaza as at La Venta. These four plazas are evenly spaced throughout the city. Their layouts are nearly identical and are likely laden with directional symbolism. Ceramics from the plazas are similar in style and technique, implying contemporaneity as well as broad social equity.

The overall message at Tres Zapotes is consistent with what we see in places like the Indus and West Africa: collective governance, power-sharing among participant groups, heterarchy rather than hierarchy. Tres Zapotes might be a concrete realization of Yoffee's (2016) social *and* physical 'infrastructures of resistance' to formal power. Yoffee emphasizes that infrastructures are social, referring to groups of people and their leaders who are not part of formal governing institutions. But the infrastructures may have also been physical. The two may have allowed Tres Zapotes to persevere through whatever external conditions brought about the decline of La Venta in 400 BCE. Tres Zapotes was very long-lived, persisting to 300 CE. The ethnic diversity of the city may have required different factions to cooperate if all were to achieve some measure of stability, resilience, and sustainability. The organizational and material design principles allowing this should be of compelling interest to urban scholars and planners today.

4.2 Valley of Mexico: Teotihuacan

Recent research on some well-known, singularly impressive and influential cities have yielded new and surprising insights about ancient urbanization, in turn suggesting the need for new concepts and theories. As noted in Section 2, the great metropolis of Teotihuacan conforms to general urban scaling laws as established by urban science. But it also represents a break in the social and cultural history of Mesoamerica. The city was of unprecedented size and population for a Mesoamerican city. It covered 20 square kilometers. The latest demographic studies establish a population of 100,000 (Smith et al., 2019).

Teotihuacan was also unprecedented in terms of its formal planning and the size and scale of its monuments (Smith, 2017). The entire city was orthogonally planned. Perhaps most significantly, it contained housing that was never seen before. This took the form of more than 2,000 modular, multifamily apartment compounds with courtyards and patios built between 250 CE and 350 CE during a phase of urban renewal. This standardized housing contained an estimated 90 percent of the city's residents (Smith et al., 2019). It may reflect a phase of *social* renewal triggered by changes in the city's governing 'social contract' that offered a greater degree of social mobility to the resident population (Stanton et al., 2023). Another planning innovation – the Avenue of the Dead aligned on a central north–south axis – served as an armature for planning civic monuments as well as the social housing. Michael E. Smith (2017) describes Teotihuacan as an 'anomaly'. The reasons behind this are much more interesting than the city's conformance to general scaling laws.

Teotihuacan was populated via immigration. Like Uruk, the city was a powerful magnet attracting people from throughout the region. Cowgill (2003) supports an earlier finding that 80–90 percent of people in the Valley of Mexico lived there. As with Uruk, the conjoined processes of extreme urbanization and ruralization must have seemed 'global' to anyone living in the region (Yoffee, 2005; Clayton, 2015). The resident population was socially heterogeneous, multiethnic, and linguistically diverse, a product of immigration from the Gulf Coast and the west (Spence et al., 2005; Sugiyama, 2022). This movement is evidenced by the existence of at least three distinctive ethnic enclaves at Teotihuacan identified on the basis of burial practices, pottery styles, and studies of human biology (York et al., 2011). The most well-known immigrant enclaves are the Oaxacan Barrio at the southwest edge of the city, the Michoacan Compound at the west edge, and the Merchants Barrio (containing Gulf Coast and Mayan peoples) to the east (Manzanilla, 2009; Manzanilla, 2017). This pattern of enclavization bears some conformance to a spatial model of the preindustrial city presented by Sjoberg (1960), in which an elite central zone was surrounded by a 'commoner zone' organized into ethnically segregated neighborhoods and containing household industries. However, there is evidence in Teotihuacan's housing compounds for ethnic mixing. Chavez and Gazzola (2021) substantiate Michoacan and Zapotec co-residence and suggest that marriage and other alliances forged across ethnic divisions promoted security and prosperity. This did not entirely eliminate tension with ethnic Teotihuacanos. However, the city's ethnic diversity clearly produced a dynamic, creative society as evidenced by the production of fine craft items and lavish sumptuary goods made from jadeite, travertine, and other exotic materials (Manzanilla, 2015).

Although as centrally planned as one city could get, there is still ample evidence at Teotihuacan for considerable citizen autonomy and control – for "bottom-up expression of local group and individual interests" (Cowgill, 2015: 127). The standardized apartment compounds varied internally in terms of furnishings and activities. They were routinely expanded, remodeled, improvised, and adjusted (Cowgill, 2015: 157). Material differences between compounds also likely expressed differences in status, class, occupation, and ethnicity (Nichols, 2016: 16). As noted, there was social and economic mixing at the neighborhood level and even within apartment compounds. Perhaps most interestingly and surprisingly, lots of informal, 'insubstantial' housing existed alongside the formal, planned apartment compounds (Clayton, 2015). Robertson (2008) suggests that as much as 15 percent of Teotihuacan's population lived in informal housing (see also Stanley et al., 2016). It also appears that citizens at Teotihuacan, unlike those at Nineveh under Sennacherib, could take liberties encroaching upon the orthogonal street grid without losing life or limb. Cowgill (2015: 157) notes that the spacious entryway of one household jogged far out into the street.

Work at Teotihuacan has produced other unexpected findings. One is that the city has a surprisingly low Gini coefficient. Early calculations put the figure at 0.12 (Kohler et al., 2017). This figure has recently been adjusted upward to a still relatively low 0.34 (Smith, 2023a: 184) and, in another calculation, 0.41 (D. Chase et al., 2023). Elites probably clustered at the center of the city and likely enjoyed the best access to city services (Dennehy et al., 2016; Stanley et al., 2016). However, the Gini values and other data suggest that there was broad economic equity, prosperity, and social mobility.

It is also surprising, given the scale and complexity of the city, that political governance of this highly ordered and multiethnic polity appears to have been more collective than autocratic. As with Indus cities, there is no evidence of royal palaces, burials, or estates (Yoffee, 2016; Smith, 2017; Carballo, 2020). There are no depictions of individual leaders or political dynasties in the civic art. Feinman and Carballo (2018; see also Feinman et al., 2023) have quantified the matter with their 'Collectivity Score'. They code polities as autocratic or collective based on measures of economic differentiation, investments in public versus private space, and the amount of individuation apparent in art, burials, and other categories of material culture. In a numerical system that scales governance from more autocratic (0) to more collective (3), Teotihuacan's Collectivity Score is a 3. This finding of collective governance squares with the conclusion of a separate study by Norwood and Smith (2022) that uses the amount of formal public open space – which is considerable at Teotihuacan – as a key measure for inferring governance regime.

Scholars vigorously debate the precise form of Teotihuacan governance (Froese and Manzanilla, 2018). Linda Manzanilla (2009, 2018) argues for governance by a council of four leaders, each representing a different quadrant of the city. This constitutes another version of the collective, heterarchical governance scheme that has been evidenced elsewhere (e.g., West Africa, the Indus). And, like those other cases, Teotihuacan clearly substantiates Jennings' (2016) belief that we need to rethink the traditional narrative about the rise of cities and civilization.

Leaders and citizens at Teotihuacan seem to have successfully harnessed diversity and cultural creativity on a collective governance model that generated wide prosperity. Almost certainly the sharing of basic cosmological beliefs had something to do with this. Teotihuacan, like the other cities considered here, combined numerous features and processes of an intercultural character that we can mine for insights relevant to open, inclusive city building today.

After Teotihuacan, urban patterns in the Valley revert to the older, ancestral pattern that was first expressed at La Venta. La Venta's Collectivity Score is 0 in Feinman and Carballo's model. The Aztecs would emulate some aspects of Teotihuacan materiality – a monumental core, orthogonal planning – to create their imperial capital at Tenochtitlan (now buried under Mexico City) after 1300 CE (Smith, 2017). Teotihuacan likely figured prominently in the Aztec creation myth, and we know that Aztecs made pilgrimages to the old city. However, Aztec governance was predicated on hierarchy and a strong ruler cult with all of the associated bells and whistles (e.g., royal palaces, elite iconography).

Interestingly, Teotihuacan-style collaborative governance seems to have been revived at the city of Tlaxcallan, a smaller, ethnically diverse polity located 60 miles east of Tenochtitlan and occupied at the same time (1300 CE to 1521 CE; see Fargher et al., 2011, Fargher et al., 2020, Fargher et al., 2022). Tlaxcallan was likely populated by refugees fleeing Aztec domination. The city was organized into twenty neighborhoods, each focused on its own small plaza and temple. Twenty-four plazas in total are distributed throughout the city and are intervisible with each other. A much larger open plaza serving the entire city is built on a massive 20,000-square-meter platform at a ceremonial center called Tizatlan located about 1 kilometer outside of town. There are no substantial pyramids at Tlaxcallan and an unambiguous 'palace' has not yet been identified. Residential areas are uniform in style and reflect minimal social differentiation.

The form of Tlaxcallan's built environment suggests a decentralized, consensus-based political system, perhaps a ruling council as proposed for Teotihuacan, with rotating leadership (Carballo, 2022). The city has a Collectivity Score of 3 in Feinman and Carballo's model. If the proposed Gini value of 0.23 based on residential land holdings is correct (Fargher et al., 2022), then there was also broad socioeconomic equality.

Fargher et al. (2022) suggest that Tlaxcaltecan citizenship extended across diverse ethnic groups, including immigrants fleeing oppression. Migrants were fully incorporated into political and legal systems. David Carballo (quoted in Wade, 2017b) suggests that the city represents "the opposite of ethnic nationalism." It was a city open to all, where a distinctive *tlaxcalteca* identity was expressed. Tlaxcallan may have been to Tenochtitlan what Tres Zapotes was to La Venta: a physical and social infrastructure of resistance to autocratic power.

4.3 Valley of Oaxaca

The ancient Zapotec capital of Monte Albán is one of the oldest cities in the Americas, dating to 500 BCE. It is also perhaps the most remarkable from a sustainability standpoint. The city's longevity or 'apogee' of 1,300 years is almost twice that of any other ancient Mesoamerican city (Feinman et al., 2022: 156; Feinman et al., 2023). This raises questions about the secret to Monte Albán's success.

The city was founded through a coalitionary process that brought multiple competing and diverse polities together in a defensible central location on a steep hilltop. In contrast to traditional models that often link longevity to strong top-down governance, longevity at Monte Albán is linked to collaborative governance (Collectivity Score = 2.5) where top and bottom work together. Feinman and coauthors see the city's origins as premised on a founding social contract that emphasized collaboration. The early locating of a large public plaza at the very top of the hill was instrumental in forging community by requiring coordinated labor for leveling the hilltop, defining the space, and constructing public buildings. Pooled labor was also required for constructing and maintaining household terraces located below the plaza, which involved constructing shared walls and other facilities.

The founding social contract was subsequently reinforced by the city's compact plan and a series of trails and footpaths that served to interconnect households and provide equitable access to public space. There was relative socioeconomic equality among households at Monte Albán as measured by a Gini value of 0.41 and a value of 0.38 for the Valley of Oaxaca as a whole (Feinman et al., 2018). The iconography at the site is similar to that found at Teotihuacan: an emphasis on representation of depersonalized, faceless individuals and collective activities and rituals.

The main plaza at Monte Albán (Figure 6) was larger than anything previously constructed in the area and was continuously remodeled over 1,300 years (Joyce, 2009). The plaza could have held most of the 17,000 people that occupied Monte Albán at its peak in around 500 CE. It became more exclusive toward the end of the Classic period (around 600 CE) with the onset of more autocratic rule and increasing class divisions.

Monte Albán also yields insight into sustainable urban agriculture. As much as we moderns might like to think so, urban agriculture is not a new thing (Smith, 2023a: 210–211). For the residents of Monte Albán and those of many other cities in the ancient world, agriculture was a fully integrated urban activity and was so for millennia (Isendahl, 2012; Chase and Chase, 2016). Water flow in the Valley of Oaxaca is neither year-round nor predictable. Monte Albán's

Figure 6 Monte Albán, Main Plaza. Photograph by Arian Zwegers, distributed under Creative Commons Attribution 2.0 Generic license.

Source: Wikimedia Commons, https://commons.wikimedia.org/wiki/File:Monte_Alban,_Main_Plaza,_Building_J,_and_the_North_Platform_(20498776500).jpg.

residents constructed and collectively maintained a system of wells, canals, dams, and reservoirs for supporting terrace agriculture. These collective investments in infrastructure contributed to long-term resilience by increasing social capital and inspiring trust (Carballo et al., 2022). Security of the food supply was likely a factor in preventing residents from moving elsewhere. Rojas and Dávila (2020) suggest that revitalizing this ancient water control system today can better serve the informal communities developing in Oaxaca City, while also 'greening' the city as a whole. Monte Albán thus provides unique, practical insights into the institutional arrangements, environmental relationships, and governance structures that promote long-term urban well-being and sustainability.

4.4 The Maya Lowlands

The Maya Lowlands encompassing parts of Mexico, Guatemala, and Belize are a particularly rich area of urban archaeological study. Like everywhere else, scholars are discovering lots of variation in the physical composition of Mayan cities and, by extension, variation in political structures, social life, and governing ideologies (see especially the contributions to Marken and Arnauld, 2023).

Classic period (200 CE to 900 CE) Tikal is one of the area's most famous cities, with an impressive monumental core, relatively high inequality as measured by a Gini value of 0.62, and evidence for named rulers. Lesser known and very different in character is the Middle Pre-Classic (900 BCE to 400 BCE) settlement of Nixtun-Ch'ich, a collectively governed city built on a grid 400 years *before* Teotihuacan. Nixtun-Ch'ich embeds in its physical plan a distinctive creation myth involving pervasive crocodile symbolism. Its gridded street system also served as a public good that drained storm water and human waste from the city (Pugh et al., 2022a, 2022b). Stoner and Stark (2022) describe low-density, distributed urban networks in the Gulf Lowlands that display a mix of governance arrangements from autocratic to collective (Stark and Stoner, 2022). Thus, Mayan cities challenge many assumed correlations between central planning, political hierarchy, and economic inequality.

What follows are more detailed descriptions of two cities whose findings scholars are particularly keen to relate to contemporary urban issues and concerns. My discussion respects two points about Maya civilization that are worth keeping in mind: first, that the greatest achievement of the Maya is not the monumental architecture that peaks through the forest canopy, but rather it was their extensive 'tropical forest urbanism' (Demarest and Victor, 2022: 776-777); and second, that the most interesting question about Mayan urban history is not why their cities 'collapsed' but rather how they managed to survive for so long in a challenging tropical environment (Smith, 2023c: 9).

4.4.1 Caracol

Diane, Arlen, and Adrian Chase's work at Caracol (Figure 7) in the southern lowlands provides a particularly comprehensive picture of Mayan urbanism (Chase and Chase, 2017; Chase, 2023). It is a picture that also lends itself to direct conceptual comparison with cities today. Caracol (600–900 CE) was the center of an expansive (200 square kilometers) and well-integrated landscape of large and small settlements, intensively cultivated agricultural terraces, and nearly 2,000 water reservoirs (Chase, 2016a). The prominence and sophistication of this agricultural landscape has earned for Caracol the moniker of a 'garden city' (Chase and Chase, 1998), after Ebenezer Howard's (1898) classic formulation. The population of the city is estimated to have been 100,000 to 115,000 at 650 CE. The population density of the downtown core is figured at 940 people per square kilometer, roughly in-between the density of modern Boston and Philadelphia (Chase 2016b: 16). The built environment consisted of a central monumental core connected by dendritic causeways to

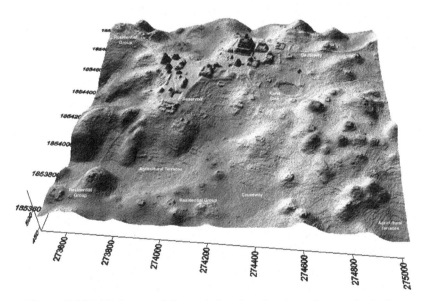

Figure 7 LIDAR image of Caracol showing the city epicenter, including monumental architecture, agricultural terraces, causeways, reservoir, and residential groups. From A. Chase et al. (2014), with permission of the primary author.

outlying settlements that the Chases, following Garreau (1991), describe as 'edge cities' (Chase and Chase, 2007). Indeed, Caracol can be seen as paradigmatic of an ancient form of 'Transit Oriented Development' that efficiently moved people and resources across the city and facilitated orderly growth and service provision as the city margins expanded (Chase, 2023).

Like Monte Albán, Caracol offers insight into sustainable urban agriculture. The city's extensive system of agricultural terraces and reservoirs conformed the settlement to its natural setting. This reflects a unique adaptation to local landscape hydrology that lacked standing bodies of water (Chase and Cesaretti, 2019). Like its neighbor Tikal (see Murtha, 2023), Caracol engineered monumental buildings to channel rainfall runoff into large holding tanks (Scarborough and Lucero, 2010; Murphy and Crumley, 2022: 32; A. Chase et al., 2022). These investments in terra-formed landscapes and civic architecture successfully adapted, and indeed pre-adapted, Mayan cities to cope with environmental variability and climate change.

Caracol's residents enjoyed equitable access to reservoirs in the urban core as well as hundreds of smaller residential reservoirs distributed around the landscape (Chase, 2019). Given the extent of this continuous 'conurban' (Garrison et al., 2019: 143) landscape, citizens would have produced most of their own food. Food deserts were unlikely, even with extensive sprawl (compare with today; see Hamidi, 2019). Markets were also evenly distributed around this landscape, with each house located within 3 kilometers of their closest local option (A. Chase et al., 2015; D. Chase and A. Chase, 2020). This arrangement guaranteed resident access to a variety of exotic goods that could not be produced locally, including obsidian (a prized volcanic glass), marine shell, salt, and jadeite. The Gini value of 0.34 for Caracol is, like Teotihuacan's, impressively low for a city of its size and scale (Chase, 2017, 2023: 357; Kohler and Smith, 2018: 294). A. Chase et al. (2020: 354) document social mixing by status and wealth over the entirety of Caracol's urban landscape.

Other objects (polychrome pottery, ritual containers, and *incensarios*) were so widely distributed that they likely reflect a common ritual (and civic) identity that helped to integrate the entire polity. This seems comparable to the veneer of widely shared material objects and symbols that characterized Indus cities. Arlen and Diane Chase take this distribution as reflecting a 'symbolic egalitarianism' that served the interests of citizens as well as their political leaders who, more likely than not, occupied a well-established administrative hierarchy but without anywhere near total power over their subjects (A. Chase and D. Chase, 2009). The Collectivity Score for Caracol is 2.0. Chase (2023:365) sees the city as occupying an intermediate point along the autocratic–collective continuum, something that is reflected by the generally "poorer" quality of its elite burials compared to counterparts at other Maya cities.

As at Mohenjo-daro and other Indus cities, Caracol's shared identity was likely instrumental in helping to generate social cohesion, civic prosperity, and overall good citizen health (D. Chase and A. Chase, 2017). The prosperous middle class at Caracol certainly challenges some of the assumptions made about premodern cities, including the popular one that they consisted of a rich elite and a vast, impoverished working population (e.g., Gilbert, 2013). The broad prosperity of Caracol's population was a function of equitable access to food, water, other social goods, and public space. Despite its dispersed character, Caracol was an eminently 'walkable' city that permitted easy access to resources and infrastructure (D. Chase et al., 2023). In fact, Caracol appears to have achieved what some leading urbanists see as needed in cities today: a polycentric, well-connected, walkable, diverse form of settlement with a good urban fabric in the suburbs (Mehaffy, 2018, 2019).

4.4.2 Chunchucmil

An ancient Mayan city as rich as Caracol with implications for urbanism today is Chunchucmil, located in northwest Yucatan. Scott Hutson, a codirector of the archaeological field research at Chunchucmil, has synthesized most of what we know about the structure and form of the city in his book *The Ancient Urban Maya: Neighborhoods, Inequality, and Built Form* (Hutson, 2016). Much of what follows is based on his synthesis.

Chunchucmil dates to the middle of the Classic period in Maya history, 400–600 CE. Its urban area covers 20–25 square kilometers. Its peak population was 40,000 to 45,000. The population density of more than 3,000 people per square kilometer in the city's 6-square-kilometer center exceeds the density of many modern cities. Some 10,000 structures have been mapped at Chunchucmil, grouped into more than 1,400 house compounds bordered by low stone walls or *albarradas*. The city lacks a single civic-ceremonial core defined by a huge temple-plaza complex, making Chunchucmil an unusual Mayan city in terms of monumental architecture. The city lacks a 'regal-ritual' character. Instead, it contains more than a dozen monumental compounds or quadrangles having modestly sized patios and temples only 6–18 meters high. These quadrangles served as civic-ceremonial focal points for several distinct residential neighborhoods. Interestingly, the quadrangles repeat on a larger scale the layout of domestic groups, a social and perhaps moral code that also characterized Mesopotamia and the Indus. Like Teotihuacan, Chunchucmil lacks freestanding carved monuments that glorify individual rulers or ruling dynasties. Its Collectivity Score of 2.5 suggests that the city was governed collaboratively (Feinman and Carballo, 2018).

Chunchucmil's relevance for contemporary urbanism is established in other ways. First, its public spaces look very secular. They are not designed to accommodate large groups of citizens or pilgrims. Second, Chunchucmil is located in an area of marginal agricultural productivity. Soils are poor, rainfall is scarce, and yields are low. Although we cannot rule out some infield agriculture (Fisher, 2014), the disconnect between agricultural marginality and high population density, plus the city's secularized character, alerts us to a different reason for its existence: as a commercial center in desirable products. These commodities likely included obsidian and especially salt. Third, the largest public space in the city is a centrally located marketplace with capacity for up to 500 stalls and 1,000 people (Hutson, 2016: 196–198). Smaller open spaces throughout the city perhaps had the same function. Various other services related to commercial activity were also likely on offer, in the areas of transportation, security, hospitality, and entertainment. Thus, if Caracol was a garden city, Chunchucmil was a market city.

Neighborhoods at Chunchucmil are clearly identifiable and arranged in a distinctive hub-and-spoke pattern radiating out from the central core (Figure 8). Raised processional avenues called *sacbes* connect monumental compounds to each other and, to some extent, to neighborhoods. Hutson argues that the hub-and-spoke plan strongly encouraged regular and intense face-to-face interaction among neighborhood residents while facilitating access to the civic-ceremonial compounds and the central marketplace. Interestingly, this radial/concentric model is akin to that characterizing the much earlier Trypillian megasites and one that would be later found in the Post-Classic Mayan city of Mayapan (Hutson and Solinis-Casparius, 2022). The public spaces (patios) at the monumental compounds were large enough to accommodate all of the residents of a particular neighborhood. The city's physical framework accomplished this without impeding the freedom of residents to circulate more widely via other streets (*callejuelas*) and pathways. The hub-and-spoke pattern and the cross-cutting pathways are reminiscent of some African settlements not considered here – for example, the Ibo of Nigeria. Their use of such a plan made for efficient use of space and increased feelings of intimacy while also offering escape from uncomfortable encounters (Hull, 1976).

As discussed previously, residential mixing by ethnicity and wealth was relatively common in ancient cities. The amount of ethnic diversity at Chunchucmil is unknown, but evidence suggests the existence of wealth differences between households. Household wealth at Chunchucmil is measured by

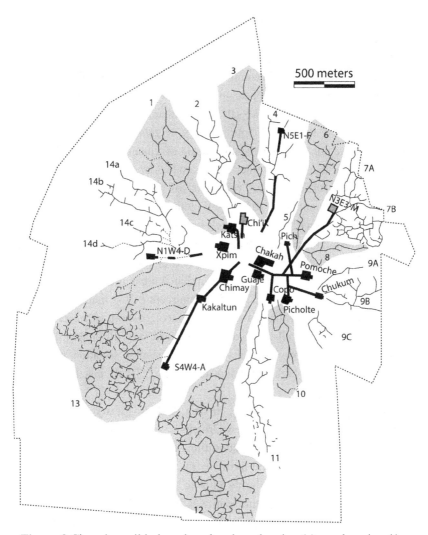

Figure 8 Chunchucmil hub-and-spoke plan, showing (a) numbered and/or shaded neighborhood 'spokes', (b) named monumental compounds as black squares and rectangles, and (c) connecting processional avenues or *sacbes* as thick black lines. Map courtesy of Scott Hutson.

architectural volume and domestic yard, or *solare*, size. The Gini values calculated by Hutson for Chunchucmil average around 0.58. These values are in line with the values that have been generated for modern cities – for example, Chicago's Gini value hovers around 0.52, St. Louis's around 0.50, and New York City's around 0.54. However, Chunchucmil seems to have avoided the residential segregation that, in our modern context, typically accompanies differences in household wealth. Detailed analysis of two neighborhoods shows that richer and poorer households lived side by side at Chunchucmil as they did at Caracol. They were connected by shared boundary walls and streets (Hutson and Welch, 2021).

Wealth differences in architectural volume and yard size notwithstanding, all households at Chunchucmil appear to have enjoyed roughly equal access to important commercial goods like salt and obsidian. These commodities were widely distributed across houselots in every neighborhood in the city. This suggests that regional commerce linked all of Chunchucmil's households, however unequal they were in other ways, into overlapping and interdependent social networks. Hutson and his coauthors call these networks 'cooperative associations' (Magnoni et al., 2014: 167). Evidence for their importance lies in the outward extension of the urban core's practice of *albarrada* construction to the city's residential periphery. Here, there was no particular need for residents to delineate houselots with stone walls. Yet they did it anyway, perhaps as a symbolic marker of shared identity (and a shared urban imaginary) with those living closer to the city center. This is reminiscent of the material 'veneers' previously described for Mohenjo-daro and Caracol. In short, whatever inequality existed at Chunchucmil was likely experienced very differently than how citizens experience urban inequality today. A similar situation may have obtained in the other high-Gini-value cities (e.g., Tikal) discussed in this Element.

Walkability, connectivity, social mixing, and prosperity are all central aspirations of today's so-called New Urbanism. Analysis of Chunchucmil in light of our contemporary urban condition suggests that the ancient Maya were effectively practicing and living by the tenets of New Urbanism – but actually realizing that paradigm's elusive goal of social and economic mixing – 1,500 years before the term was invented by Western architects and planners (Hutson and Welch, 2021). Chunchucmil successfully realized every one of the Charter of the New Urbanism's (Congress for the New Urbanism, 2000) basic principles:

- A "coherent and supportive physical framework" (p. 339) with clearly defined neighborhoods and corridors.
- Neighborhoods "diverse in use and population" (p. 339).
- "Universally accessible public spaces and community institutions" (p. 339).
- A "regional economy that benefits people of all incomes" (p. 340).
- "Citizen-based participatory planning and design" (p. 339), reflected by the freedom that Chunchucmil's residents apparently had to make bottom-up decisions about *albarrada* and *callejuela* construction and the use of open space.

Thus, Chunchucmil nicely illustrates several formal aspects of an open, inclusive city as manifested in the ancient world: low walls, permeable edges, ample pathways, and coproduced public space.

4.5 North America: Cahokia and Chaco Canyon

In his article "Civilization in Color: The Multicultural City in Three Millennia," Xavier de Souza Briggs (2004) compellingly argues that our best historical examples of well-functioning pluralist cities are ancient Rome and medieval Córdoba. Both were shaped by explicit commitments to cosmopolitan city building. These commitments were driven, however, by autocratic rule. I have already discussed several ancient examples of diverse, intercultural cities that were developed on collective or collaborative grounds. Some of them are separated by vast amounts of space and time: Mohenjo-daro in the Indus Valley and Teotihuacan in the Valley of Mexico. North America is notable for having two good examples based on the definition of city used in this Element: the great earthen mound site of Cahokia in the Mississippi River Valley near St. Louis and the great sandstone building complex of Chaco Canyon on the Colorado Plateau in northwest New Mexico. Both were active at approximately the same time, roughly 1000 CE to 1150 CE.

The residents of Cahokia were ancestral to Eastern Woodlands Indigenous groups – those at Chaco to contemporary Pueblo peoples of the American Southwest. There is good evidence based on studies of material culture and human biology that both Cahokia and Chaco were multiethnic polities (for Cahokia, see Alt, 2006; Emerson and Hedman, 2016; for Chaco, see Schillaci, 2003; Wills, 2009; Heitman and Plog, 2015; Lekson, 2018). Cahokia is unambiguously urban with a relatively high-density core, while Chaco is more like a low-density megasite. Not everyone is buying into the urban status of one or both of these settlements. Storey (2020: 133–135) presents Cahokia and Chaco as "disputed cases," and Woolf (2020) is also unsure. Jennings (2016) identifies Cahokia as a city that never really flourished as one. My view is that both qualify and have something to teach us about city building today.

Cahokia was a sprawling metropolis covering 20 square kilometers and containing huge, conical and platform mounds and clearly differentiated public space (Figure 9). Like the Avenue of the Dead at Teotihuacan, the Rattlesnake Causeway served as a central, north–south baseline for planning a citywide grid of houses, public buildings, and other features (Baires, 2022: 25). Cahokia housed up to 20,000 people (Pauketat and Alt, 2015; Pauketat et al., 2015). As at Teotihuacan, many of those residents were immigrants from elsewhere who were attracted by the city's power. But unlike Teotihuacan, Cahokia does

Figure 9 Artist's conception of Cahokia. Image by Herb Roe, distributed under Creative Commons Attribution-Share Alike 4.0 International license.

Source: Wikimedia Commons, https://commons.wikimedia.org/wiki/File: Cahokia_Aerial_HRoe_2015.jpg.

not conform to laws of urban scaling (Peregrine et al. 2014). This does not necessarily mean that it is an 'anomaly' (Pauketat et al., 2023), only that something distinctive in the history of urbanism was taking place there.

Cahokia sits in an environment of very rich agricultural potential at the nexus of many riverine exchange corridors. However, the bigger draw for residents was likely socioreligious. At its height between 1100 CE and 1200 CE, tens of thousands of people covering an area of 30,000 square kilometers identified with Cahokia (Pauketat, 2019). The city created an impact felt even farther afield, and perhaps constituted North America's first urban 'megaregion'. Cahokia was comparable in size to its contemporaries London and Paris. The Mesoamerican archaeologist John Clark notes that if you found Cahokia in the Mayan Lowlands its urban status would not be in doubt; indeed, "it would be a top 10 of all Mesoamerican cities" (quoted in Lawler, 2011:1619).

Chacoan urbanism is centered on a collection of twelve, multistory sandstone masonry 'Great Houses' containing hundreds of rooms each located in a narrow, roughly 16-kilometer-long canyon. The Great Houses are intervisible with each other, but the urban landscape extends well beyond this 'Downtown Chaco' core. A sustaining hinterland contains up to 300 outlying masonry pueblos of similar architectural style. The farthest outlier is 250 kilometers away from the central canyon. The entire network of settlements was connected by 650 kilometers of roadways. This road network covered the entire Four Corners area of the American Southwest where the states of Colorado, Utah, Arizona, and New Mexico converge. About 2,500 people lived full-time in the downtown core and 60,000 to 100,000 more plugged into the network over 100 square kilometers. This distribution of settlements easily gives Caracol a run for its money as an example of a complex, networked landscape. In fact, Lekson (2018) uses the term *altepetl*, borrowed from Mesoamerican archaeology (see Hirth, 2008), to insist that Chaco was a bona fide city. *Altepetl* is an urban form distinguished by a central capital surrounded by up to 75 square kilometers of farmland and governed on a rotating or shared basis that prevented development of hereditary claims to rulership.

The earthen mounds at Cahokia and the sandstone Great Houses at Chaco are clearly monumental. They were arranged and sequenced in coherent spatial patterns, involving principles of cardinality and keyed to the movement of the sun, moon, and perhaps other heavenly bodies. These features were built out of the landscape rather than imposed on it; i.e., Cahokian platform mounds emulate Mississippi River Valley bluffs while Chacoan Great Houses emulate Colorado Plateau mesas. What Pauketat (2020b: 97,106) says about Cahokia also goes for Chaco: it was a "living, breathing urban hybrid of people and other-than-human beings," an "ontological tangle of history and humanity." These cityscapes likely materialized mythic narratives about ancestral origins and the relationship of people to the cosmos. They were theatrical exercises: visual and auditory assaults on the senses that produced in their users (immigrants at Cahokia; mostly pilgrims at Chaco) exactly the kinds of 'affective' experiences that cognitive scientists see as critical for good architecture and good urbanism. The Métis architect and scholar David Fortin (2022) offers an Indigenous perspective on Cahokia: it provided the urban dweller with a shared sense of purpose and cosmological connectivity. I think the same can be said for Chaco. It is interesting that Fritz (1978) identifies specific forms of 'rotating symmetry' in the ritual architecture of Chaco Great Houses and also among Great Houses at a regional scale that may be a symbolic reflection of cosmological beliefs as well as a commitment to *altepetl* forms of rotating governance.

It is intriguing that both Cahokia and Chaco powered up as urban phenomena right around the time that Córdoba was enjoying its 'Golden Century', i.e., between 929 CE and 1031 CE. It has always struck me that there was something in the air during this century and the one immediately following (what might be called the 'Long Twelfth Century', 1050 CE to 1200 CE) that propelled cultures in North America and elsewhere toward long-distance interactions and inspired local investments in monumental placemaking. That 'something' is still rather elusive. However, all scholars would agree that power and ceremony at both Cahokia and Chaco were intertwined in significant ways. Each place had an allure or mystique that made people want to be there and motivated them to travel long distances to do so.

The specific governance structures associated with Cahokian and Chacoan urbanism are not entirely clear. In some models they are highly centralized polities run by autocratic leaders who used a combination of ideology and political force (or at least the threat of violence) to maintain social order (on Cahokia, see Tainter, 2019; on Chaco, Stuart, 2000). In other models they are communal undertakings based on shared, deeply compelling 'Big Ideas' and forms of political power that are rather more fluid and heterarchical. Pauketat (2019: 103) describes the cultural orders of Cahokia and Chaco as "open and permeable" (on Chaco collectivity, see also Mills, 2023). This may have been part of their cosmopolitan appeal. But even scholars preferring the communal alternative recognize that both cultures were organizationally quite complex, perhaps of a kind unknown in history either before or after.

The built environment of each settlement was, from time to time, contested. Cahokia's central Grand Plaza was a dynamic public space. Its surrounding palisade expanded and contracted several times over the city's history, suggesting that struggles over space could erupt at any time. According to recent geophysical studies (Stauffer et al., 2023), Cahokia's plaza provided "eclectic settings for diverse behaviors that likely ranged from the clandestine to the spectacular" (p. 361). The Indigenous (Ohkay Owingeh) writer Rebecca Roanhorse (cited in Newitz, 2021: 252) uses Cahokia in her storytelling because of its complexity and cosmopolitanism, which included political rivalries and conflicts both internal and external. For Roanhorse, these urban qualities humanize the ancestors and narrow the gap between past and present. Chaco had its own dynamic of complex and shifting relationships, culminating in the end with the previously open Great Houses being completely enclosed by stone walls.

The most interesting studies of Cahokian and Chacoan governance use empirical evidence to suggest that these urban phenomena were not so much distinct political entities as 'pluralities' or 'hybridities' characterized by great cultural and ethnic diversity and integrated by novel ideologies and practices. This was likely a function of their geographical reach, which extended south to the Basin of Mexico and contact with the Toltec Empire – and its great capital city of Tula, which flourished between the heydays of Teotihuacan and Tenochtitlan – and other Mesoamerican cultures. The precise integrative aspects of Cahokian and Chacoan Big Ideas are tough to determine archaeo-logically. However, it is a good bet that they were rooted in animism and world renewal rituals and spiced up by the long-distance connections with urban centers in Mesoamerica.

More apparent is the intercultural effects of these ideas. Citizens of both Cahokia and Chaco successfully harnessed ethnic, linguistic, and other cultural diversities to make dramatic and unprecedented investments in place. Open, permeable cultural orders spurred long-distance trade and exchange and sup-ported prosperous ways of living. There are echoes here of Swahili and other open city urbanisms. The current challenge to Cahokian and Chacoan archae-ology is to discover the unifying ideas and commitments that forged common-ality out of diversity and its associated forms of spatial belonging. What were the norms of ethnic coexistence? How were they established? How did they encourage (or compel) what Briggs (2004) describes as the "cross-cutting loyalties" that bridge ethnic difference, promote collective action, and defuse social conflict?

Even if we eventually discover these norms of ethnic coexistence there is no guarantee that Cahokian or Chacoan history will have any general lessons to teach us about urbanization today. Some lessons have already been proposed. Tainter (2019) uses Cahokia to warn about the dangers of top-down, elite-driven urbanism that does not benefit ordinary people. Stuart (2006) cites Chacoans for choosing an uncontrolled growth trajectory that led to overexploited farmland, loss of community, and the inability to deal with climatic catastrophe. The message from both is doom and gloom, whereas the story is likely a bit more complicated.

At the very least Cahokia and Chaco can be heralded for offering unique kinds of urban experiences – created with a respect for cultural diversity and reverence for local ecology – whose principles might inspire a new kind of urban planning sensibility today. Cahokian and Chacoan planners were, in fact, posthumanists, new materialists, and more-than-human thinkers before those concepts became fashionable (Jon, 2020). Pauketat (2020b: 102) sug-gests that Cahokia raises theoretical questions about the nature of urbanism – specifically, about the 'affective properties' of a region and their importance in designing built environments that reflect place and promote sustainability. Chaco does the same. Houston et al. (2018: 197) capture the relevance of both North and Mesoamerican urbanisms in a nutshell: "On a planet where urban life is driving planetary change and is conditioned by it, re-enchanting urban connectivities through multispecies relationships is a vital component of refiguring rights to the city and finding ethical, just and inclusive forms of urban planning."

5 Planning Lessons for the Twenty-First-Century City

This section draws together threads identified in previous sections and summarizes some lessons of ancient urbanism that can benefit comparative urban studies scholarship and practices of urban placemaking today. As Michael E. Smith notes (2009, 2019), any findings and insights from archaeology that relate to contemporary planning and policy will have to be expressed in ways that allow urban studies scholars, planning professionals, and policymakers to translate them into familiar terms. They must be brought into the same 'frame of reference' (Smith 2023a: 1).

5.1 General Lessons for Comparative Scholarship

The most basic lesson of this Element is that there is significant idiosyncratic variation in the physical planning of ancient cities and the social processes by which they were organized. Sections 3 and 4 offer just a small sampling of this variation. In surveying first cities from a global perspective, it is clear that a wide range of planning and design possibilities were present at the very beginning of urbanization, and even within the same geographical area (e.g., Mesopotamia, the Maya Lowlands). Interventions came from the top and percolated up from the bottom – what Michael E. Smith (2011) refers to as centralized and 'generative' planning, respectively. Citizens across the social spectrum exercised agency in shaping their built environments. Official and insurgent (Ortiz, 2023) practices of city building produced both orthogonal and organic patterns, each reasonably seen as the product of evolved minds interacting with local circumstances (Ramzy, 2016). Successful cities offered affective experiences that made people want to be there despite the difficulties and challenges of living with difference. Diversities in urban form and governance set conditions that helped create diverse historical trajectories of development. Thus, the notion of ancient cities as 'bold social experiments' (Graeber and Wengrow, 2021: 4) certainly applies (see also Jennings, 2016; Murphy and Crumley, 2022; Yoffee, 2022; Kim and McAnany, 2023).

Given the variety and intensity of urbanizing processes in the distant past it is clear that we need to reject today's widely expressed claim that we are living in an 'Urban Age', or what Geoffrey West (2018) refers to as the 'Urbanocene'. The Urban Age thesis was promulgated in 2008 when it was determined that most people on the planet were now living in cities. Such conceptions distance the present from the past in ways that are unhelpful. They imply that little if anything can be learned from the past that relates to urbanism today. As Monica L. Smith (2019: 243) notes, archaeological evidence indicates that past eras sometimes had higher percentages of the population living in cities than we do today. There were times in ancient Mesopotamia when 75 percent of the population lived in cities. By contrast, Woolf (2020) predicts that we moderns will not reach the 75 percent figure until the end of this century. Might knowledge of earlier Urban Ages help us prepare?

Archaeology substantiates that living with great urban diversity is nothing new. Ethnic and/or class heterogeneity characterized neighborhoods in ancient cities where residential areas have been systematically excavated, including Mesopotamia, along the East African coast, at Teotihuacan, and in the Maya Lowlands. Certainly, relatively homogeneous ethnic barrios and enclaves were also part of the mix. The ancients harnessed diversity's advantages to increase prosperity and generate equitable and sustainable urban communities. Even where there was social inequality in access to space and services (as measured by high Gini coefficients), people still enjoyed some measure of guaranteed access to basic resources, as documented by the study of diets and skeletons. Social mixing combined with guaranteed access to basic resources almost certainly had something to do with creating the robust middle-class existences that are evident, in different forms, in cities like Caracol and Chunchucmil.

The ancients held what can only be described as progressive attitudes about immigration and immigrants. Attitudes toward immigration are detected in one of its primary material signatures, informal housing. Informality – a mode of urbanization that occurs outside formal legal structures and processes (see the compilation of perspectives in Porter, 2011) – is a topic of great interest to contemporary urban planners and policymakers (McGuirk, 2014: 25). The amount of informal housing that existed in ancient cities – some of which had central core densities comparable to those of today – appears to have been substantial. The various contexts of this housing suggest that citizenship in the cities considered here (especially Teotihuacan, Tlaxcallan, and Songo Mnara) was predicated on Henri Lefebvre's (1996) notion of *inhabitance* – living there – rather than on cultural group or immigration status. Today's widely discussed 'Right to the City' – another Lefebvrian concept that is central to the United Nations' New Urban Agenda where it deals with inclusion and equity – was thus more or less guaranteed. Informal housing was located in the interstices of public and private space, between elite structures, and up against dividing walls. Despite being in full view of elites, such informal housing did not appear to threaten what we might call 'local property values'. What else might we discover if we investigated the open spaces *between* palaces, temples, and pyramids? Perhaps such spaces were not always given over to parks and gardens (Stark, 2014). We might acquire some clues about how to better provide "unregulated dwelling environments" (Peattie, 1994: 136) under conditions of urban densification (McGranahan et al., 2016) or better ways to implement

'Lean Urbanism': bottom-up city building that is unencumbered by onerous building and zoning codes (Dittmar and Kelbaugh, 2019).

5.2 Design Principles for Urban Planning and Placemaking

More specific lessons from the ancients relate to design principles for planning and placemaking. The contemporary urban theorist and planner Richard Sennett (2018) discusses a menu of planning practices into which those of the ancients can fit and that further archaeological research might supplement and expand. His framework is predicated on a vision or model of the city as an 'open system', credited to Jane Jacobs and her classic work (Jacobs, 1961). The open city is intercultural and cosmopolitan (Saitta, 2020). It is predicated on intellectual and aesthetic receptivity to different people, places, and experiences (Noble, 2013). It emphasizes empathy, toleration, and respect for other cultures and values (Werbner, 2014: 307).

Sennett proposes five design principles – what he calls 'open forms' – for producing the cosmopolitan city. The first principle is *synchronous public spaces* that accommodate many activities at once, and thereby draw people in. The second principle is *porous edges*, or borders. Borders contrast with boundaries, which are nonporous. Depending on context, walls can be either borders or boundaries. Jacobs (1961: 267), drawing upon Kevin Lynch (1960), made a similar contrast between 'seams' and 'barriers'. Jacobs' notion of seam as a "line of exchange along which two areas are sewn together" (p. 267) has much in common with Sennett's notion of the porous edge or border. The third principle is *place markers*: monuments, murals, and other objects that punctuate the cityscape. Sennett describes them as 'exclamation points' (focal points) that declare the importance of a space. The fourth principle is the *shell*: material forms whose possibilities are not exhausted by a configuration imposed at the start. The final principle is *seed planning*: using these various forms in different ways in different contexts like a farmer uses seed in different environmental circumstances to achieve a desired outcome. Seed planning is pitched as an alternative to master planning. It works through small projects and with local community collaboration, an approach that allows maximum room for variation and innovation. The analogy with agriculture is apt for the purposes of this study because we have seen how the ancients often integrated the urban and rural in ways that ensured wider civic prosperity and sustainability.

As evidenced by the case studies presented in this Element, the ancients worked with all of these design principles and forms to promote cosmopolitan placemaking. They combined them in innovative ways that supported inclusive 'cultures of citizenship' (Merrifield, 2014) and long-term cultural and environmental sustainability. The huge open spaces at the heart of Trypillian settlements were obviously synchronous in nature. The design of open access public space in much later, more compact urban settlements ran the gamut from a single huge plaza at Monte Albán to the distributed or polycentric infrastructures evident at Chunchucmil and Tlaxcallan. Mesoamerican plazas were multifunctional and had the capacity to accommodate citizens at whatever scale was appropriate: neighborhood, district, quadrant, and sometimes even the entire city (Norwood and Smith, 2022: 942–943). These collaborative investments in shared and equitably distributed infrastructure had enduring benefits that fostered more inclusive and resilient cities (Carballo et al., 2022: 15). Plazas at Tlaxcallan are especially notable: they intermixed politics, religion, and commerce in ways that did not discriminate by ethnicity or gender (Fargher et al., 2022).

Songo Mnara is exemplary for its provision of synchronous public spaces that enhanced its cosmopolitan character. By all accounts the city was an enticing place that invited social mixing. Songo Mnara is also remarkable for its interdigitation of public and private space. In this regard it is reminiscent of today's Latino or Barrio Urbanism (Diaz, 2005; Diaz and Torres, 2012). These placemaking efforts merge private and public spaces (front yards, streets) in ways that support informal economies, sociability, and neighborhood cohesion. They also promote health and well-being. Sandoval-Strausz (2019) notes how Latino cityscapes made a difference to residents surviving the Chicago heatwave of July 1995, in which temperatures climbed to 106 degrees Fahrenheit (41 degrees Celsius) and stayed there for a week. The differential survival rate between ethnic groups for this period is striking: Latinos experienced only 9 heat-related deaths, whereas African Americans suffered 256 and Anglos 252 (Klinenberg, 2002). Sandoval-Strausz suggests that Latino residential practices – by encouraging residents to seek shade out of doors and the company of neighbors and friends on sidewalks and storefronts – were crucial to their survival. In this case the urban built environment was particularly determinative in its effects. This manifestation of built form is the product of 'syncretic processes' (Arreola, 1988: 310) that combine a number of cultural influences including Roman, Islamic, Iberian, and Native Mesoamerican. The example nicely illustrates what can be a very close articulation between urban cultural identity, materiality, prosperity, and survivability.

Edges were used at Mohenjo-daro to anchor spaces of everyday exchange and civic inculcation. In this respect the city produced the equivalent of today's 'cosmopolitan canopies' (Anderson, 2011). Edges were most likely the locations of markets in Mesopotamia (McMahon, 2013a). Walls were employed as permeable or porous borders in the Indus (Kenoyer, 2003) as well as in East Africa. They facilitated the construction of informal housing by providing one stable sidewall for temporary structures.

The standardized apartment compounds or 'housing estates' (Wengrow, 2018) at Teotihuacan qualify as shells in Sennett's sense. They were apparently shaped and renovated to their occupants' desires. Teotihuacan's social housing is reminiscent of the 'incremental housing' promoted by the Pritzker Prize–winning architect Alejandro Aravena, who has used open-form shells to develop public housing for the poor in his homeland of Chile and elsewhere (Kimmelman, 2016). Teotihuacan's social housing was done on a scale and with the kind of quality that rivals that of contemporary Vienna, which is exemplary among cities in the Global North for successfully addressing the world's equitable housing crisis (Kadi and Lilius, 2022). The open space at Khorsabad, and the empty spaces in urban fabrics that are apparent elsewhere in the ancient world (see Smith, 2008), may have been shells at a larger scale. Only further archaeological investigation will disclose how these open spaces were infilled and used. The Mayan cities of Chunchucmil and Caracol bring together a number of Sennett's open city elements: low walls, porous borders, many pathways, and accessible public plazas. Their built environments offered freedom of movement and many opportunities for social interaction and mixing.

Other innovative ideas are conceivably embedded in the design and construction of public buildings and monuments, described by Sennett as place markers. Some of these seem to incorporate patterned complexity and various optical refinements that cognitive scientists suggest play important evolutionary roles in exciting our evolved sensibilities and stimulating our brains (Goldhagen, 2017). Many ancient buildings, monuments, and public spaces were invested with affective qualities and narrative power via their positioning in urban material assemblages: the city as theatrical exercise (see Alt and Pauketat, 2020). Most intriguing is the palace at Khorsabad (McMahon, 2013b), and we see something similar at Babylon (Van de Mieroop, 2003). The Americas are replete with examples of how ancient builders located stone pyramids, earthen mounds, and masonry Great Houses to heighten emotional and psychological responses, tell stories, preserve memories, and create mystery while at the same time producing social integration and a shared civic identity. We do this today (e.g., design proposals for rebuilding lower Manhattan after the 9/11 attacks), and there are many studies of the experiential nature of architecture in the Western tradition (e.g., Coburn et al., 2017). But perhaps there are new principles of design to be illuminated if we allow that 'built narrative' (Filep et al., 2014) is a practice much more deeply rooted in the human past.

Thus, all things considered, the first cities were 'seed planned' by citizens in ways that promoted equity, sociability, and intercultural integration. Sennett's forms, and perhaps others still to be defined, are embedded in the built environments of ancient cities, awaiting discovery and analysis. I believe that they have something to teach us today that can inform new urban imaginaries, models, and practices of city building.

5.3 Developing Urban and Peri-urban Agro-ecologies

Cities today are increasingly concerned with securing food and water supplies. Spaces and skills related to both are vanishing (Barthel and Isendahl, 2013). We are seeing major investments in green buildings with 'vertical farms' that double as sites of food production. City planners are looking at rooftops, empty office buildings, and other unused spaces as potential sites of food production (O'Brien, 2023; Yeung, 2023).

The ancients pioneered strategies and technologies that embedded agriculture in the urban fabric (Figure 10). There was wide distribution and intimate folding of agricultural plots into the urban landscape at Caracol, and likely in Mesopotamian cities as well (Van de Mieroop, 1997: 86). Mayan cities across the board provide a basis for reimagining urban–rural relationships today (Isendahl and Smith, 2013; Garrison et al., 2019; Marken and Arnauld, 2023). Monte Albán provides opportunities to learn from (1) worldviews that deeply respected water and (2) their associated technologies of water control (Rojas and Dávila, 2020). The floating gardens (*chinampas*) of the ancient Aztec capital of Tenochtitlan are often cited as another agricultural technology that could be resurrected for contemporary application (Ebel, 2020). The same sort of facility with managing nature likely accompanied urbanization at Jenné-jeno. Ancient 'sponge cities' (Meddeb and Hanforth, 2022) of Africa and the Americas offer contemporary cities new imaginaries for reintroducing agriculture as an urban and peri-urban (Simon and Adam-Bradford, 2016) function and practicing it in inclusive and sustainable ways.

Another question to which ancient urbanism can speak concerns the virtues and vulnerabilities of local versus regional food-sourcing systems. Isendahl (2022) argues that food self-sufficiency is not synonymous with sustainability. He draws attention to the difference between Caracol's locally focused system of growing food and Tikal's regionally based and centrally managed system for importing food. This contrast raises the intriguing question of which system is least vulnerable to perturbations. The question is still open for us moderns. Like Isendahl, Fisher (2020: 417) urges a long-term, comparative perspective on ancient cities that can clarify the interconnected social and environmental dynamics underlying agricultural sustainability.

5.4 Urban Governance: Toward Equity and Inclusion

The case studies discussed in this Element substantiate claims that stable collaborative urban governance has a long history and wide distribution across the ancient world. Founding social contracts and attendant moral codes based on collaboration are clearly evidenced in Mesoamerica and they are implicated in Mesopotamia, the Indus, and Africa. There is ample and widespread evidence for citizen-based participatory design in the ancient city – for political arrangements that allow individuals and interest groups wide latitude to codesign and coproduce the city without much, if any, interference from planning elites or government bureaucrats. Indeed, informality appears to have been the original default setting for urbanization in human history.

Population density was not an obstacle to citizen-based participatory planning and design. Some of the densest neighborhoods in the ancient world were also the most egalitarian (Carballo and Feinman, 2016). There is also compelling evidence that the more collective the governance of these cities, the more resilient and durable they were. Fargher et al. (2022) put an even finer point on the matter by favorably comparing Tlaxcallan to classical Athens in terms of political philosophy and its materialization. For Fargher and colleagues, the ancient world challenges Eurocentric thinking about the uniqueness of the West in promoting democratic principles of urban governance and demonstrates greater success in living by them. This work warrants interrogating the ancient city for embedded governance principles and practices that produce equity, prosperity, and sustainability. We now have a variety of hierarchical and heterarchical governance systems stacked under the lab table in close to equal numbers. There are likely other forms out there yet to be recognized (Crumley, 2021).

5.5 Sacred Civics vs. Smart Cities

Twenty years ago, Leonie Sandercock (2003: 225) ended her widely respected book *Cosmopolis II* by suggesting that it might be time to reintroduce the importance of the sacred, or spirit, into our thinking about cities and their natural settings. There is no better source of ideas than Indigenous cultures and epistemologies. It seems that the Maya and other Mesoamerican cultures made no theoretical or practical distinction between urban and rural, and their cosmology emphasized a conservationist ethic (Lucero, 2018). Ancient city planners were sensitive to local environmental conditions and used history, art, iconography, monumentality, and wider 'sacred landscapes' to create a shared civic identity out of cultural diversity and thereby promote a long-term, just sustainability. The veneers of Indus Valley cities and the symbolic

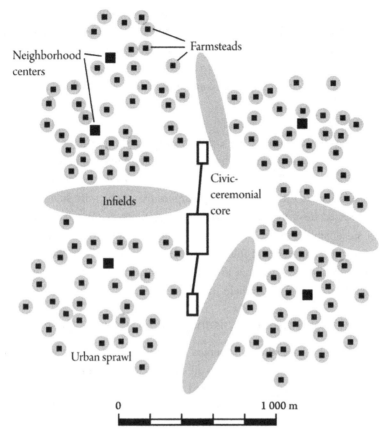

Figure 10 Schematic model of Classic Maya urban agro-ecology.
Urban sprawl was interspersed with garden areas around each farmstead.
Larger open spaces were devoted to short-fallow or permanent agriculture.
Garden and farming areas are shaded. From Barthel and Isendahl (2013),
with permission of the authors.

egalitarianism of the Mayan city of Caracol embody ideas and 'cosmovisions' that put citizens on the same page, helping to contain more destructive polarizations and tensions.

Today, ideas about the sacred city are receiving book-length treatment. Engle et al. (2022) propose 'sacred civics' as a paradigm for city building that resurrects and redeems Indigenous values of mutuality, collectivity, equity, sustainability, and accountability to nature. They suggest that Indigenous worldviews provide a look at "emancipatory social and civic infrastructure" and that these and other values are "manifest in the public spaces, buildings, institutions, and arteries of commerce, trade, mobility, and connectivity of urban centers" (Chung-Tiam-Fook et al., 2022: 39, 33). This extends the critical urban theorist Arturo Escobar's call for a 're-sacralization' of urban design (Escobar, 2022b). Cahokia – given its stunning geographical reach and, especially, its refusal to behave according to typical urban scaling laws – may end up being one of our better guides for creating a sacred, sustainable, more-than-human city.

Ben Wilson (2020: 46) notes that while the residents of Mohenjo-daro and other Indus Valley cities built their communities on a reverence for water (as did the Cahokians), we moderns are building ours on a faith in the digital future. Robert Sampson (2017) critiques the 'smart city' focus on technology and Big Data as solutions to urban problems. He argues that, to be truly smart, cities of the future need fresh theoretical ideas and analytic tools for relating environmental sustainability to the promotion of human welfare. The challenges are cultural and in some sense spiritual. While in recent years some of the bloom has gone off the smart city rose, it is still not clear what kind of faith will replace it. A sacred civics paradigm can help frame the choices.

5.6 Urban Trajectories: Is the Future City Low-Density?

It is clear from the case studies presented in this Element that there are multiple pathways of urban change evident in the ancient world. Some experiments in urbanism explicitly rejected what had come before (e.g., Tres Zapotes, Tlaxcallan). Others retrieved what had been lost (e.g., the Teotihuacan Revival at Tenochtitlan). Some contemporary urbanists argue that modernity's condition of sprawling metropoli is no longer sustainable and that cities today need to contract and densify (e.g., Kunstler, 2011). Others argue that the urban future is dispersed and low-density, with all kinds of alternative settlement forms destined to fill the periphery (Soja, 2018).

This question has prompted an interesting debate among archaeologists. The ancients planned with landscape in mind, viewing settlement systems as assemblages of human and nonhuman elements. They often eschewed the urban–rural binary, a rejection that in fact anchors current 'planetary urbanization' theorizing (see Brenner, 2019 and many references therein). Scarborough and Isendahl (2020) highlight the socio-environmental benefits of low-density, tropical urban systems in an era of climate change. They suggest that we can learn from their resource base diversity, regional interconnectivity, and adaptive flexibility. Likewise, Murphy and Crumley (2022: 88) see low-density urbanism as an effective and durable strategy if combined with urban infield agriculture. On the other hand, Fletcher (2019) expresses reservations about the long-term resilience of low-density urbanism. He suggests that the implications are "ominous" because today's low-density urban forms, in contrast to contemporary high-density forms, do not derive from any *local* ancient precedents.

The debate is unresolved. But if sprawling, low-density urbanism is the future, the study of ancient forms encompassing agricultural areas, industry, open spaces, wetlands, and forests may produce better conceptual tools for managing and analyzing it (Hawken and Fletcher, 2021; Canuto and Estrada Bella, 2022). Herein lies another reason why today's fashionable 'Urban Age' thesis is counterproductive for comparative analysis.

5.7 The End of Cities: Is Urban Collapse Inevitable?

Any discussion of the ancient city is obliged to engage with the popular topic of urban 'collapse'. A vast scholarly and popular literature exists on the topic (McAnany and Yoffee, 2010; Middleton, 2017; Newitz, 2021). Traditional explanations invoke war, climate change, ecocide, famine, disease, and more. The notion of collapse may be overdone; what we interpret as collapse may in fact be social reorganization or reconfiguration (see also M. L. Smith, 2019: 253–259). In the Maya Lowlands, D. Chase et al. (2023) note that the famous Classic period collapse was followed by a Postclassic period characterized by smaller, more densely occupied cities in new locations. The descendants of the ancient Lowland Maya are still with us today. The same goes for descendants of the Ancestral Pueblo of Chaco Canyon, who did not 'mysteriously disappear' according to popular culture and many National Park Service tourism brochures. We know where the ancestors went, and we wear the remains of their ancient cities as a pedigree of urban legitimacy (M. L. Smith, 2019: 253). Empirically, there is as much historical evidence for settlement persistence as for settlement failure (Smith et al., 2021; D. Chase et al. 2023).

That said, the case studies discussed in this Element implicate a collapse narrative that squares with existing data *and* serves as a cautionary tale for modern times. The wheels started coming off at Tres Zapotes when autocratic rule began reasserting itself at 300 CE. Rising social inequality and emerging authoritarian leadership spelled an end to collective governance and widespread prosperity at Teotihuacan (Clayton, 2015: 295–296; Cowgill, 2015: 235; Manzanilla, 2015; Freixa, 2018). The same goes for Monte Albán (Feinman et al., 2022). A broadly similar story about political conflict can be told for Caracol (A. Chase and D. Chase, 2007: 231, 2009: 21; Chase, 2023; D. Chase and A. Chase, 2014; see also Jennings, 2016: 230) and perhaps even settlements throughout the Gulf Lowlands (Stark and Stoner, 2022).

In today's post–George Floyd era of rising race-based tensions, it is worth pointing out that it was not the existence of urban ethnic diversity per se that caused ancient cities to disintegrate, although in some cases governance structures might have done more to dampen segregation and better manage conflict (e.g., on Cahokia see Emerson and Hedman, 2016). In this regard, Yoffee and Seri (2019) make a compelling point that when cities like Uruk and Teotihuacan fell it was the central administrative precincts that were destroyed, while the neighborhoods where diversities lived and thrived remained untouched. Lucero et al. (2011) offer something of the same for the Terminal Classic Maya: centers fell, but rural peripheries persisted through the collapse. Although central administrative hierarchies are fragile and neighborhoods resilient, we have evidence that the ancient Maya were able to articulate new relationships between cosmology, governance, and the built environment even through episodes of civic collapse (Mixter, 2019). Therein lies some hope for cities dealing with ethnic conflict today.

6 Summary and Conclusion

This Element has taken a 9,000-year global tour of what we know about the first cities – their physical forms, governance structures, and historical trajectories – viewing them as experiments in equitable, prosperous, and sustainable urbanism. It has considered the ancient urban world much as scholars have considered the urbanized Global South and cities in other marginalized geographies: as a "generative source of theoretical innovation and comparative insight" (Brenner, 2019: 45). We have viewed the urban past in much the same way that Fisher (2020: 420), quoting the poet and environmental activist Wendell Berry, views the agricultural past: as "a resource, a fund of experience, a lexicon of proven possibilities and understood mistakes." I have been centrally concerned with the relationship between urban built form and cosmopolitan, sustainable placemaking. In so doing I have sought to enlarge the sample of cities that can be used to build urban theory, enrich scholarly debates, inspire new imaginaries of what the city can be, and develop a transdisciplinary, comparative urbanism (Baumanova and Vis, 2020; Akbar et al., 2021; Smith, 2023a: 245–246).

Archaeological study of the first cities indicates that today's urban growth is not unprecedented. Ancient cities were embedded in global (for their time) relationships and processes. Archaeological knowledge reaffirms the wisdom of challenging traditional evolutionary narratives about the appearance and historical sequencing of the city, the state, monumental infrastructures, intensive agricultural landscapes, and other material trappings of civilization. It also reaffirms the wisdom of challenging popular accounts of human history that see the past as a prelude to a predetermined or inevitable present.

The first cities were shaped by significant migrations of culturally diverse peoples and, in many cases, successfully integrated these immigrant diversities. Shared commitments were cultivated to produce new forms of 'social and spatial belonging' being urged by theorists of the multi- or intercultural city (Sandercock, 2003; Wood and Landry 2008; Saitta, 2020; Engle et al., 2022). These processes were assisted by architectures and built landscapes that tapped into humankind's shared nature and common evolved sensibilities. Successful integration of cultural diversity fueled civic creativity and socioeconomic prosperity.

Governance of ancient cities covered the waterfront between heterarchical and hierarchical, with collective arrangements for exercising authority showing up in some really surprising places. The evidence substantiates Graeber and Wengrow's (2021: 4) inference that the past presents a "carnival parade of political forms" that testify to human agency and creativity. Urban size, scale, and density do not appear to have been obstacles to the development of collective governance, and collective governance appears to have promoted long-term resilience and sustainability.

Overall, ancient cities generated what Ash Amin (2008: 20) calls 'urban plenitude': a collective domain of public spaces, local facilities, well-functioning infrastructures, and shared experiences. The ancients were experts in using all of Sennett's open design forms to promote inclusive, cosmopolitan cities. They engineered landscapes and developed land use and resource management strategies that could cope with vagaries of climate and environmental change. It is becoming increasingly clear that these ancient urban practices were not only sustainable but in many cases *regenerative*: conscious of and geared toward renewing the city's place in a larger living ecosystem (Gibbons, 2020; Camrass, 2023). It seems that there is not much that is novel in any of the popular urbanisms that currently surround us, whether called Smart, Creative, Green, Sustainable, Regenerative, or, especially, 'New' urbanism. The ancients experimented with city planning and design principles and strategies that anticipated most of what exists in all contemporary urbanisms. If other principles and strategies exist – which they almost certainly do – they are likely best detected using a methodology of engaged pluralism.

Although ancient cities were successful by any number of criteria, it is of course important to keep in mind that they were as contradictory and paradoxical as cities of today. They were often crowded, chaotic, dirty, smelly, noisy places, prone to infectious disease and conflict (see Algaze, 2018 and commentaries therein). They concentrated wealth, centralized power, and nurtured intolerance. Their built environments were complicit in dividing, excluding, and oppressing citizens. They could be environmentally destructive. There can be no returning to an idyllic urban past that never existed. Nonetheless, like cities of today, ancient cities were always wellsprings of possibility (Beauregard, 2018; Graeber and Wengrow, 2021).

Archaeological knowledge demonstrates significant commonalities and significant differences between the cities of the deep past and the cities of today. Whether there are lessons in this body of archaeological knowledge for practicing urban planners, policymakers, designers, and architects is an open question. A significant obstacle are assumptions by those unfamiliar with the 'Ancient Urban Other' that the past does not matter or that ancient city building simply cannot be comparable to urbanism today. There is good potential if we stay focused on *general* principles and strategies, work comparatively across multiple cases, and act on a small-scale via seed planning or what the visionary urbanist Jaime Lerner described as 'urban acupuncture' (Lerner, 2014). The last fifty years of research on humankind's first cities have gone a long way toward fulfilling Richard Ford's vision of how archaeology can better serve society. This should increase our confidence that relevant lessons of the past can be identified and applied today in ways that generate greater urban equity, prosperity, and sustainability.

References

Agyeman, J. (2013). *Just Sustainabilities: Policy, Planning, and Practice.* London: Zed Books.

Akbar, N., Abubakar, I., Shah, A., and Al-Madani, W. (2021). Ecological embeddedness in the Maya built environment: Inspiration for contemporary cities. *Land*, 10(12), 1360–1389. https://doi.org/10.3390/land10121360.

Algaze, G. (2018). Entropic cities: The paradox of urbanism in ancient Mesopotamia. *Current Anthropology*, 59(1), 23–54.

Alt, S. (2006). The power of diversity: The roles of migration and hybridity in culture change. In B. Butler and P. Welch, eds., *Leadership and Polity in Mississippian Society.* Carbondale, IL: Center for Archaeological Investigations, pp. 289–308.

Alt, S. and Pauketat, T., eds. (2020). *New Materialisms Ancient Urbanisms.* London: Routledge.

Amin, A. (2006). The good city. *Urban Studies*, 43(5–6), 1009–1023.

Amin, A. (2008). Collective culture and urban public space. *City*, 12(1), 5–24.

Anderson, E. (2011). *The Cosmopolitan Canopy: Race and Civility in Everyday Life.* New York: W. W. Norton & Company.

Arreola, D. (1988). Mexican American housescapes. *Geographical Review*, 78(3), 299–315.

Asomani-Boateng, R. (2011). Borrowing from the past to sustain the present and the future: Indigenous African urban forms, architecture, and sustainable urban development in contemporary Africa. *Journal of Urbanism*, 4(3), 239–262.

Badger, E. (2019). What a Nobel laureate discovers at Burning Man. *The New York Times*, September 8: B1.

Baires, S. (2022). *Cahokia and the North American Worlds.* Cambridge: Cambridge University Press.

Baker, H. (2023). The later phases of Southern Mesopotamian urbanism: Babylonia in the second and first millennia BC. *Journal of Archaeological Research*, 31(2), 147–207. https://doi.org/10.1007/s10814-022-09174-8.

Bard, K. (2008). Royal cities and cult centers, administrative towns, and workmen's settlements in ancient Egypt. In J. Marcus and J. Sabloff, eds., *The Ancient City: New Perspectives on Urbanism in the Old and New Worlds.* Santa Fe, NM: School for Advanced Research Press, pp. 165–182.

Barnes, T. and Sheppard, E. (2010). "Nothing includes everything": Towards engaged pluralism in anglophone economic geography. *Progress in Human Geography*, 34(2), 193–214.

Barthel, S. and Isendahl, C. (2013). Urban gardens, agriculture, and water management: Sources of resilience for long-term food security in cities. *Ecological Economics*, 86, 224–234.

Batty, M. (2022). Review of L. Bettencourt, *Introduction to Urban Science: Evidence and Theory of Cities as Complex Systems. Papers in Regional Science*, 101(2), 505–508.

Baumanova, M. (2020). *Urban Public Space in Colonial Transformations*. Cham: Springer Nature.

Baumanova, M. (2022). Transitory courtyards as a feature of sustainable urbanism on the East African coast. *Sustainability*, 14(3), 1759. https://doi.org/ 10.3390/su14031759.

Baumanova, M. and Vis, B. (2020). Comparative urbanism in archaeology. In *Encyclopedia of Global Archaeology*. Cham: Springer. https://doi.org/ 10.1007/978-3-319-51726-1_3478-1.

Beauregard, R. (2018). *Cities in the Urban Age: A Dissent*. Chicago, IL: University of Chicago Press.

Berg, N. (2011). Burning Man and the metropolis. *Places Journal*, January [online]. https://placesjournal.org/article/burning-man-and-the-metropolis/? cn-reloaded=1.

Bettencourt, L. (2021). *Introduction to Urban Science: Evidence and Theory of Cities as Complex Systems*. Cambridge, MA: MIT Press.

Bettencourt, L. and G. West (2010). A unified theory of urban living. *Nature*, 467(7318), 912–913.

Bissell, W. (2018). The modern life of Swahili stonetowns. In S. Wynne-Jones and A. LaViolette, eds., *The Swahili World*. London: Routledge, pp. 589–601.

Blanton, R. and Fargher, L. (2008). *Collective Action in the Formation of Pre-modern States*. New York: Springer.

Box-Steffensmeier, J. (2022). Engaged pluralism: The importance of commitment. *Perspectives on Politics*, 20(1), 9–21.

Brenner, N. (2019). *New Urban Spaces: Urban Theory and the Scale Question*. New York: Oxford University Press.

Briggs, X. de S. (2004). Civilization in Color: The Multicultural City in Three Millennia. *City & Community*, 3(4), 311–342.

Camrass, K. (2023). Regenerative urbanism: A causal layered analysis. *Foresight*, 25(4), 502–515. https://doi.org/10.1108/FS-11-2021-0227.

Canuto, M. and Estrada-Belli, F. (2022). Patterns of early uranism in the Southern Maya Lowlands. In M. Love and J. Guernsey, eds., *Early Mesoamerican Cities: Urbanism and Urbanization in the Formative Period*. Cambridge: Cambridge University Press, pp. 73–98.

Carballo, D. (2020). Power, politics, and governance at Teotihuacan. In K. Hirth, D. Carballo, and B. Arroyo, eds., *Teotihuacan: The World beyond the City*. Washington, DC: Dumbarton Oaks, pp. 57–96.

Carballo, D. (2022). Governance strategies in precolonial central Mexico. *Frontiers in Political Science*, 4, 797331.

Carballo, D. and Feinman, G. (2016). Cooperation, collective action, and the archaeology of large-scale societies. *Evolutionary Anthropology*, 25(6), 288–296.

Carballo, D., Feinman, G., and López Corral, A. (2022). Mesoamerican urbanism: Indigenous institutions, infrastructure, and resilience. *Urban Studies*. https://journals.sagepub.com/doi/10.1177/00420980221105418.

Chapman, J. (2017). The standard model, the maximalists, and the minimalists: New interpretations of Trypillia mega-sites. *Journal of World Prehistory*, 30(3), 221–237.

Chapman, J., Gaydarska, B., and Nebbia, M. (2019). The origins of Trypillian megasites. *Frontiers in Digital Humanities* 6(10). https://doi.org/10.3389/fdigh.2019.00010.

Chase, A. S. Z. (2016a). Beyond elite control: Residential reservoirs at Caracol, Belize. *Wiley Interdisciplinary Reviews: Water*, 3(6), 885–897.

Chase, A. S. Z. (2016b). Districting and urban services at Caracol, Belize: Intra-site boundaries in an evolving Mayan culture. *Research Reports in Belizean Archaeology*, 13, 15–28.

Chase, A. S. Z. (2017). Residential inequality among the ancient Maya: Operationalizing household architectural volume at Caracol, Belize. *Research Reports in Belizean Archaeology*, 14, 31–39.

Chase, A. S. Z. (2019). Water management among the ancient Maya: Degrees of latitude. *Research Reports in Belizean Archaeology*, 16, 101–109.

Chase, A. S. Z. (2023). Urban planning at Caracol, Belize: Governance, residential autonomy, and heterarchical management through time. In D. Marken and M. Arnauld, eds., *Building an Archaeology of Maya Urbanism: Planning and Flexibility in the American Tropics*. Denver: University Press of Colorado, pp. 349–376.

Chase, A. S. Z. and Cesaretti, R. (2019). Diversity in ancient Maya water management strategies at Caracol, Belize and Tikal, Guatemala. *Wiley Interdisciplinary Reviews: Water*, 6e1332.

Chase, A. and Chase, D. (1998). Scale and intensity in Classic Period Maya agriculture: Terracing and settlement at the "Garden City" of Caracol, Belize. *Culture & Agriculture*, 20(2–3), 60–77.

Chase, A. and Chase, D. (2007). Ancient Maya urban development: Insights from the archaeology of Caracol, Belize. *Belizean Studies*, 29(2), 60–72.

Chase, A. and Chase, D. (2009). Symbolic egalitarianism and homogenized distributions in the archaeological record at Caracol, Belize: Method, theory, and complexity. *Research Reports in Belizean Archaeology*, 6, 15–24.

Chase, A. and Chase, D. (2016). The ancient Maya city: Anthropological landscapes, settlement archaeology, and Caracol, Belize. *Research Reports in Belizean Archaeology*, 13, 3–14.

Chase, A., Chase, D., Awe, J. et al. (2014). The use of LiDAR in understanding the Ancient Maya landscape: Caracol and Western Belize. *Advances in Archaeological Practice*, 2(3), 208–221.

Chase, A., Chase, D., and Chase, A. S. Z. (2020). The Maya city of Caracol, Belize: The integration of an anthropogenic landscape. In S. Hutson and T. Arden, eds., *The Maya World*. Abingdon: Routledge, pp. 344–363.

Chase, A., Chase, D., and Chase, A. S. Z. (2022). Caracol, Belize, and Tikal, Guatemala: Ancient Maya human–nature relationships and their sociopolitical context. In J. Larmon, L. Lucero, and F. Valdez Jr., eds., *Sustainability and Water Management in the Maya World and Beyond*. Boulder: University Press of Colorado, pp. 143–170.

Chase, A., Chase, D., Horlacher, T., and Chase, A. S. Z. (2015). Markets among the ancient Maya: The case of Caracol, Belize. In E. King, ed., *The Ancient Maya Marketplace: The Archaeology of Transient Space*. Tucson: University of Arizona Press, pp. 226–250.

Chase, B., Ajithprasad, P., Rajesh, S., Patel, A., and Sharma, B. (2014). Materializing Harappan identities: Unity and diversity in the borderlands of the Indus civilization. *Journal of Anthropological Archaeology*, 35, 63–78.

Chase, D. and Chase, A. (2014). Path dependency in the rise and denouement of a Classic Maya city: The case of Caracol, Belize. *Anthropological Papers of the American Anthropological Association*, 24(1), 142–154.

Chase, D. and Chase, A. (2017). Caracol, Belize, and changing perceptions of ancient Maya society. *Journal of Archaeological Research*, 25(3), 185–289.

Chase, D. and Chase, A. (2020). The ancient Maya economic landscape of Caracol, Belize. In M. Masson, D. Freidel, and A. Demarest, eds., *The Real Business of Ancient Maya Economies: From Farmers' Fields to Rulers' Realms*. Tallahassee: University Press of Florida, pp. 132–148.

Chase, D., Lobo, J., Feinman, G. et al. (2023). Mesoamerican urbanism revisited: Environmental change, adaptation, resilience, persistence, and collapse. *PNAS*, 120(31), e2211558120.

Chavez, S. and Gazzola, J. (2021). Interaction, ethnicity, and subsistence strategies among the minority groups of the ancient city of Teotihuacan. In C. Lauriers and T. Murakami, eds., *Teotihuacan and Early Classic Mesoamerica*. Boulder: University Press of Colorado, pp. 74–102.

Childe, V. G. (1950). The urban revolution. *Town Planning Review*, 21(1), 3–17.

Chirikure, S. (2020). Shades of urbanism(s) and urbanity in pre-colonial Africa: Towards Afro-centred interventions. *Journal of Urban Archaeology*, 1, 49–66.

Chung-Tiam-Fook, T., Engle, J., and Agyeman, J. (2020). Awakening seven generation cities. In J. Engle, J. Agyeman, and T. Chung-Tiam-Fook, eds., *Sacred Civics: Building Seven Generation Cities*. Oxford: Routledge, pp. 33–41.

Chwałczyk, F. (2020). Around the Anthropocene in eighty names: Considering the Urbanocene proposition. *Sustainability*, 12(11), 4458–4533.

Clark, G. (2016). *Global Cities: A Short History*. Washington, DC: Brookings Institution.

Clark, P., ed. (2013). *The Oxford Handbook of Cities in World History*. Oxford: Oxford University Press.

Clayton, S. (2015). Teotihuacan: An early urban center in its regional context. In N. Yoffee, ed., *Early Cities in Comparative Perspective: 4000 BCE–1200 CE*. Cambridge: Cambridge University Press, pp. 1–24.

Coburn, A., Vartanian, O., and Chatterjee, A. (2017). Buildings, beauty, and the brain: A neuroscience of architectural experience. *Journal of Cognitive Neuroscience*, 29(9), 1521–1531.

Congress for the New Urbanism (2000). Charter of the New Urbanism. *Bulletin of Science, Technology and Society*, 20(4), 339–341.

Cowgill, G. (2003). Teotihuacan: Cosmic glories and mundane needs. In M. L. Smith, ed., *The Social Construction of Ancient Cities*. Washington, DC: Smithsonian Institution, pp. 37–55.

Cowgill, G. (2004). Origins and development of urbanism: Archaeological perspectives. *Annual Review of Anthropology*, 33, 525–549.

Cowgill, G. (2015). *Ancient Teotihuacan: Early Urbanism in Central Mexico*. Cambridge: Cambridge University Press.

Cox, K. and Evenhuis, E. (2020). Theorizing in urban and regional studies: Negotiating generalization and particularity. *Cambridge Journal of Regions, Economy and Society*, 13(3), 425–442.

Creekmore, A. (2014). The social production of space in third-millennium cities of upper Mesopotamia. In A. Creekmore and K. Fisher, eds., *Making Ancient Cities: Space and Place in Early Urban Societies*. Cambridge: Cambridge University Press, pp. 32–73.

Creekmore, A. and Fisher, K., eds. (2014). *Making Ancient Cities: Space and Place in Early Urban Societies*. Cambridge: Cambridge University Press.

Crumley, C. (1995). Heterarchy and the analysis of complex societies. In R. Ehrenreich, C. Crumley, and J. Levy, eds., *Heterarchy and the Analysis of Complex Societies.* Washington, DC: Archaeological Papers of the American Anthropological Association 6, pp. 1–5.

Crumley, C. (2021). Preface. In T. Thurston and M. Fernández-Götz, eds., *Power from Below in Premodern Societies: The Dynamics of Political Complexity in the Archaeological Record.* Cambridge: Cambridge University Press, pp. xiii–xv.

Davis, M. (2017). The Harappan 'veneer' and the forging of urban identity. In D. Frenez, G. Jamison, R. Law, M. Vidale, and R. Meadow, eds., *Walking with the Unicorn: Social Organization and Material Culture in Ancient South Asia.* Oxford: Archaeopress Publishing, pp. 145–160.

Demarest, A. and Victor, B. (2022). Constructing policy to confront collapse: Ancient experience and modern risk. *Academy of Management Perspectives,* 36(2), 768–800.

Dennehy, T., Stanley, B., and Smith, M. E. (2016). Social inequality and access to services in premodern cities. *Anthropological Papers of the American Anthropological Association,* 27(1), 143–160.

Der, L. and Issavi, J. (2017). The urban quandary and the 'mega-site' from the Çatalhöyük perspective. *Journal of World Prehistory,* 30(3), 189–206.

Diachenko, A. and Menotti, F. (2017). Proto-cities or non-proto-cities? On the nature of Cucuteni-Trypillia mega-sites. *Journal of World Prehistory,* 30(3), 207–219.

Diaz, D. (2005). *Barrio Urbanism: Chicanos, Planning, and American Cities.* New York: Routledge.

Diaz, D. and Torres, R., eds. (2012). *Latino Urbanism: The Politics of Planning, Policy, and Redevelopment.* New York: New York University Press.

Dittmar, H. and Kelbaugh, D. (2019). Lean urbanism is about making small possible. In M. Arefi and C. Kickert, eds., *The Palgrave Handbook of Bottom-Up Urbanism.* Cham: Palgrave Macmillan, pp. 67–82.

Dovey, K. and Pafka, E. (2016). The science of urban design? *Urban Design International,* 21(1), 1–10.

Dufton, J. (2022). How do you solve a problem like the city? *Journal of Roman Archaeology,* 35(1), 351–371.

Düring, B. (2013). The anatomy of a prehistoric community: Reconsidering Çatalhöyük'. In J. Birch, ed., *From Prehistoric Villages to Cities: Settlement Aggregation and Community Transformation.* New York: Routledge, pp. 24–43.

Ebel, R. (2020). Chinampas: An urban farming model of the Aztecs and a potential solution for modern megalopolis. *HortTechnology,* 30(1), 13–19.

Emberling, G. (2015). Mesopotamian cities and urban process, 3500–1600 BCE. In N. Yoffee, ed., *Early Cities in Comparative Perspective: 4000 BCE–1200 CE.* Cambridge: Cambridge University Press, pp. 253–278.

Emerson, T. and Hedman, K. (2016). The dangers of diversity: The consolidation and dissolution of Cahokia, native North America's first urban polity. In R. Faulseit, ed., *Beyond Collapse: Archaeological Perspectives on Resilience, Revitalization, and Transformation in Complex Societies.* Carbondale, IL: Center for Archaeological Investigations, pp. 147–175.

Engle, J., Agyeman, J., and Chung-Tiam-Fook, T., eds. (2022). *Sacred Civics: Building Seven Generation Cities.* Oxford: Routledge.

Escobar, A. (2019). Habitability and design: Radical interdependence and the re-earthing of cities. *Geoforum*, 101, 132–140.

Escobar, A. (2022a). Reframing civilization(s): From critique to transitions. *Globalizations*. https://doi.org/10.1080/14747731.2021.2002673.

Escobar, A. (2022b). On the ontological metrofitting of cities. e-flux [online]. www.e-flux.com/architecture/where-is-here/453886/on-the-ontological-metrofitting-of-cities/.

Fargher, L., Antorcha-Pedemontea, R., Espinoza, V. et al. (2020). Wealth inequality, social stratification, and the built environment in Late Prehispanic Highland Mexico: A comparative analysis with special emphasis on Tlaxcallan. *Journal of Anthropological Archaeology*, 58. https://doi.org/10.1016/j.jaa.2020.101176.

Fargher, L., Blanton, R., Espinoza, V. et al. (2011). Tlaxcallan: The archaeology of an ancient republic in the New World. *Antiquity*, 85(327), 172–186.

Fargher, L., Blanton, R., and Heredia Espinoza, V. (2022). Collective action, good government, and democracy in Tlaxcallan, Mexico: An analysis based on demokratia. *Frontiers in Political Science*, 4, p.832440. https://doi.org/10.3389/fpos.2022.832440.

Farhat, G., ed. (2020). *Landscapes of Preindustrial Urbanism.* Washington, DC: Dumbarton Oaks.

Feinman, G., Blanton, R., Nicholas, L., and Kowalewski, S. (2022). Reframing the foundation of Monte Albán. *Journal of Urban Archaeology*, 5, 155–175.

Feinman, G. and Carballo, D. (2018). Collaborative and competitive strategies in the variability and resiliency of large-scale societies in Mesoamerica. *Economic Anthropology*, 5(1), 7–19.

Feinman, G. and Carballo, D. (2019). The scale, governance, and sustainability of central places in pre-Hispanic Mesoamerica. In L. Lozny and T. McGovern, eds., *Global perspectives on Long Term Community Resource Management: Studies in Human Ecology and Adaptation.* Cham: Springer Nature, pp. 235–253.

Feinman, G., Carballo, D., Nicholas L., and Kowalewski, S. (2023). Sustainability and duration of early central places in prehispanic Mesoamerica. *Frontiers in Ecology and Evolution*, 11, 076740. https://doi.org/10.3389/fevo.2023.1076740.

Feinman, G., Faulseit, R., and Nicholas, L. (2018). Assessing wealth inequality in the pre-Hispanic Valley of Oaxaca. In T. Kohler, and M. E. Smith, eds., *Ten Thousand Years of Inequality: The Archaeology of Wealth Differences.* Tucson: University of Arizona Press, pp. 262–288.

Fernández-Armesto, F. (2013). Latin America. In P. Clark, ed., *The Oxford Handbook of Cities in World History.* Oxford: Oxford University Press, pp. 364–382.

Filep, C., Thompson-Fawcett, M., and Rae, M. (2014). Built narratives. *Journal of Urban Design,* 19(3), 298–316.

Fisher, C. (2014). The role of infield agriculture in Maya cities. *Journal of Anthropological Archaeology,* 36, 196–210.

Fisher, C. (2020). Archaeology for sustainable agriculture. *Journal of Archaeological Research,* 28(3), 393–441.

Fleisher, J. (2010). Swahili synoecism: Rural settlements and town formation on the Central East African coast, AD 750–1500. *Journal of Field Archaeology,* 35(3), 265–282.

Fleisher, J. (2014). The complexity of public space at the Swahili town of Songo Mnara, Tanzania. *Journal of Anthropological Archaeology,* 35, 1–22.

Fleisher, J. and Wynne-Jones, S. (2012). Finding meaning in ancient Swahili spatial practices. *African Archaeological Review,* 29(2–3), 171–207.

Fletcher, R. (2019). Trajectories to low-density settlements past and present: Paradox and outcomes. *Frontiers in Digital Humanities.* 6, 14. https://doi .org/10.3389/fdigh.2019.00014.

Ford, R. (1973). Archaeology serving humanity. In C. Redman, ed., *Research and Theory in Current Archaeology.* New York: John Wiley and Sons, pp. 83–94.

Fortin, D. (2022). Lessons from Cahokia: Indigeneity and the future of the settler-city. In K. Ruckstuhl, I. Nimatuj, J-A McNeish, and N. Postero, eds., *The Routledge Handbook of Indigenous Development.* London: Routledge, pp. 392–401.

Fox, S. and Goodfellow, T. (2022). On the conditions of 'late urbanisation'. *Urban Studies,* 59(10), 1959–1980.

Freixa, M. (2018). Rethinking monumentality in Teotihuacan, Mexico. In A. Brysbaert, V. Klinkenberg, A. Gutiérrez Garcia-M, and I. Vikatou, eds., *Constructing Monuments, Perceiving Monumentality, and the Economics of Building: Theoretical and Methodological Approaches to the Built Environment.* Leiden: Sidestone Press, pp. 219–241.

Fritz, J. (1978). Paleopsychology today: Ideational systems and human adaptation in prehistory. In C. Redman, ed., *Social Archeology: Beyond Subsistence and Dating.* New York: Academic Press, pp. 37–59.

Froese, T. and Manzanilla, L. (2018). Modeling collective rule at ancient Teotihuacan as a complex adaptive system: Communal ritual makes social hierarchy more effective. *Cognitive Systems Research*, 52, 862–874.

Fulminante, F. (2021). Editorial: Where do cities come from and where are they going to? *Frontiers in Digital Humanities*, 7, 633838. https://doi.org/10.3389/fdigh.2020.633838.

Garreau, J. (1991). *Edge City: Life on the New Frontier*. New York: Doubleday.

Garrison, T., Houston, S., and Firpi, O. (2019). Recentering the rural: Lidar and articulated landscapes among the Maya. *Journal of Anthropological Archaeology*, 53, 133–146.

Gaydarska, B. (2016). The city is dead! Long live the city! *Norwegian Archaeological Review*, 49(1), 40–57.

Gaydarska, B. (2019). "If we want things to stay as they are, things will have to change": The case of Trypillia. In S. Kadrow and J. Müller, eds., *Habitus? The Social Dimension of Technology and Transformation*. Leiden: Sidestone Press, pp. 47–69.

Gaydarska, B. (2021). Fragmenting Trypillian megasites: A bottom-up approach. In T. Thurston and M. Fernández-Götz, eds., *Power from Below in Premodern Societies: The Dynamics of Political Complexity in the Archaeological Record*. Cambridge: Cambridge University Press, pp. 40–60.

Gaydarska, B. and Chapman, J. (2022). *Megasites in Prehistoric Europe: Where Strangers and Kinsfolk Meet*. Cambridge: Cambridge University Press.

Gayadarska, B., Millard, A., Buchanan, B., and Chapman, J. (2023). Place and time at Trypillia mega-sites. *Journal of Urban Archaeology*, 7, 115–145.

Geertz, C. (1973). *The Interpretation of Cultures*. New York: Basic Books.

Gibbons, L. (2020). Regenerative – the new sustainable? *Sustainability*, 12(13), 5483. https://doi.org/10.3390/su12135483.

Gilbert, A. (2013). Poverty, inequality, and social segregation. In P. Clark, ed., *The Oxford Handbook of Cities in World History*. Oxford: Oxford University Press, pp. 683–699.

Goldhagen, S. (2017). *Welcome to Your World: How the Built Environment Shapes Our Lives*. New York: HarperCollins.

Goodspeed, R. (2022). Review of L. Bettencourt, *Introduction to Urban Science: Evidence and Theory of Cities as Complex Systems. Journal of the American Planning Association*, 88(4), 591–592.

Graeber, D. and Wengrow, D. (2021). *The Dawn of Everything: A New History of Humanity*. New York: Farrar, Straus and Giroux.

Green, A. (2018). Mohenjo-Daro's small public structures: Heterarchy, collective action, and a re-visitation of old interpretations with GIS and 3D modelling. *Cambridge Archaeological Journal*, 28(2), 205–223.

Green, A. (2021). Killing the priest-king: Addressing egalitarianism in the Indus civilization. *Journal of Archaeological Research*, 29(2), 153–202.

Green, A. (2022). Of revenue without rulers: Public goods in the egalitarian cities of the Indus civilization. *Frontiers in Political Science*, 4, 823071. https://doi.org/10.3389/fpos.2022.823071.

Grinsell, S. (2020). The city is a lie. *Aeon*, July 30 [online]. https://aeon.co/essays/cities-are-a-borderland-where-the-wild-and-built-worlds-meet.

Gyucha, A., ed. (2019). *Coming Together: Comparative Approaches to Population Aggregation and Early Urbanization*. Albany: State University of New York Press.

Hall, T., Kardulias, N., and Chase-Dunn, C. (2011). World-systems analysis and archaeology: Continuing the dialogue. *Journal of Archaeological Research*, 19(3), 233–279.

Hamidi, S. (2019). Urban sprawl and the emergence of food deserts in the USA. *Urban Studies*, 57(8), 1660–1675.

Hammer, E. (2022). Multi-centric, marsh-based urbanism at the early Mesopotamian city of Lagash (Tell al-Hiba, Iraq). *Journal of Anthropological Archeology*, 68, p.101458.

Hammer, E., Stone, E., and McMahon, A. (2022). The structure and hydrology of the early dynastic city of Lagash (Tell Al-Hiba) from satellite and aerial images. *Iraq*, 84, 103–127.

Harding, A. (2018). The question of 'proto-urban' sites in later prehistoric Europe. *Origini: The Prehistory and Protohistory of Ancient Civilizations*, 42, 317–338.

Hawken, S. and Fletcher, R. (2021). A long-term archaeological reappraisal of low-density urbanism: Implications for contemporary cities. *Journal of Urban Archaeology*, 3, 29–50.

Heitman, C. and Plog, S., eds. (2015). *Chaco Revisited: New Research on the Prehistory of Chaco Canyon, New Mexico*. Tucson: University of Arizona Press.

Hildebrand, G. (1999). *Origins of Architectural Pleasure*. Berkeley: University of California Press.

Hirth, K. (2008). Incidental urbanism: The structure of the Prehispanic city in Central Mexico. In J. Marcus and J. Sabloff, eds., *The Ancient City: New Perspectives on Urbanism in the Old and New World*. Santa Fe, NM: SAR Press, pp. 273–297.

Hoch, C. (2022). Planning imagination and the future. *Journal of Planning Education and Research*, p.0739456X221084997.

Hodder, I. (2006). *The Leopard's Tale: Revealing the Mysteries of Çatalhöyük*. London: Thames & Hudson.

Hodder, I. and P. Pels (2010). History houses: A new interpretation of architectural elaboration at Çatalhöyük. In I. Hodder, ed., *Religion in the Emergence of Civilization: Çatalhöyük as a Case Study*. Cambridge: Cambridge University Press, pp. 163–186.

Hofmann, R., Müller, J., Shatilo, L. et al. (2019). Governing Tripolye: Integrative architecture in Tripolye settlements. *PLoS ONE*, 14(9), p.e0222243. https://doi.org/10.1371/journal.pone.0222243.

Houston, D., Hillier, J., MacCallum, D., Steele, W., and Byrne, J. (2018). Make kin, not cities! Multispecies entanglements and becoming-world in planning theory. *Planning Theory*, 17(2), 90–212.

Howard, E. (1898). *Garden Cities of To-morrow*. London: Sonnenschein & Company.

Hull, D. (1976). *African Cities and Towns before the Conquest*. New York: W. W. Norton & Company.

Hutson, S. (2016). *The Ancient Urban Maya: Neighborhoods, Inequality, and Built Form*. Gainesville: University Press of Florida.

Hutson, S., Chase, A. S. Z., Glover, J. et al. (2023). Settlement scaling in the northern Maya Lowlands: Human-scale implications. *Latin American Antiquity*, 1–8. https://doi.org/10.1017/laq.2022.103.

Hutson, S. and Welch, J. (2021). Old urbanites as new urbanists? Mixing at an ancient Maya city. *Journal of Urban History*, 47(4), 812–831.

Hutson, S. and Solinis-Casparius, R. (2022). Streets and open spaces: Comparing mobility and urban form at Angamuco and Chunchucmil, Mexico. *Ancient Mesoamerica*, 34(2), 338–359. https://doi.org/10.1017/S095653612100047X.

Huvila, I., Dallas, C., Toumpouri, M., and Enqvist, D. (2022). Archaeological practices and societal challenges. *Open Archaeology*, 8(1), 296–305.

Isendahl, C. (2012). Investigating urban experiences, deconstructing urban essentialism. *UGEC Viewpoints*, 8, 25–28.

Isendahl, C. (2022). How do we get out of this mess? Landscape legacies, unintended consequences, and trade-offs of human behavior. In J. Lamon, L. Lucero, and F. Valdez, eds., *Sustainability and Water Management in the Maya World and Beyond*. Boulder: University Press of Colorado, pp. 228–243.

Isendahl, C. and Smith, M. E. (2013). Sustainable agrarian urbanism: The low-density cities of the Mayas and Aztecs. *Cities*, 31, 132–143.

Izdebski, A. (2022). What stories should historians be telling at the dawn of the Anthropocene? In A. Izdebski, J. Halson, and P. Filipkowski, eds., *Perspectives on Public Policy in Societal Environmental Crises: What the Future Needs from History*, Cham: Springer, pp. 9–19.

Jacobs, J. (1961). *The Death and Life of Great American Cities*. New York: Vintage.

Jennings, J. (2016). *Killing Civilization: A Reassessment of Early Urbanism and Its Consequences*. Albuquerque: University of New Mexico Press.

Jennings, J. and Earle, T. (2016). Urbanization, state formation, and cooperation: A reappraisal. *Current Anthropology*, 57(4), 474–493.

Jennings, J., Frenette, S., Harmacy, S., Keenan, P., and Maciw, A. (2021). Cities, surplus, and the state: A re-evaluation. *Journal of Urban Archaeology*, 4, 15–31.

Jervis, B., Cembrzynski, P., Fleisher, J., Tys, D., and Wynne-Jones, S. (2021). The archaeology of emptiness? *Journal of Urban Archaeology*, 4, 221–246.

Jon, I. (2020). Deciphering posthumanism: Why and how it matters to urban planning in the Anthropocene. *Planning Theory*, 19(4), 392–420.

Joyce, A. (2009). The main plaza of Monte Albán: A life history of place. In B. Bowser and M. Zedeño, eds., *The Archaeology of Meaningful Places*. Salt Lake City: University of Utah Press. pp. 32–52.

Kadi, J. and Lilius, J. (2022). The remarkable stability of social housing in Vienna and Helsinki: A multi-dimensional analysis. *Housing Studies*. https://doi.org/10.1080/02673037.2022.2135170

Keith, K. (2003). The spatial patterns of everyday life in Old Babylonian neighborhoods. In M. L. Smith, ed., *The Social Construction of Ancient Cities*. Washington, DC: Smithsonian Institution, pp. 56–80.

Kenoyer, J. (2003). Uncovering the keys to the lost Indus civilization. *Scientific American*, 289(1), 66–75.

Kenoyer, J., Price, T., and Burton, J. (2013). A new approach to tracking connections between the Indus Valley and Mesopotamia: Initial results of strontium isotope analyses from Harappa and Ur. *Journal of Archaeological Science*, 40(5), 2286–2297.

Kim, N. and McAnany, P. (2023). Experimenting with large-group aggregation. *Journal of Urban Archaeology* 7, 17–30.

Kimmelman, M. (2016). Alejandro Aravena, the architect rebuilding a country. *New York Times*, May 23.

Klinenberg, E. (2002). *Heat Wave: A Social Autopsy of Disaster in Chicago*. Chicago, IL: University of Chicago Press.

Klinenberg, E. (2018). *Palaces for the People: How Social Infrastructure Can Help Fight Inequality, Polarization, and the Decline of Civic Life*. New York: Crown.

Kohler, T. and Smith, M. E., eds. (2018). *Ten Thousand Years of Inequality: The Archaeology of Wealth Differences*. Tucson: University of Arizona Press.

Kohler, T., Smith, M. E., Bogaard, A. et al. (2017). Greater post-Neolithic wealth disparities in Eurasia than in North America and Mesoamerica. *Nature*, 551(7682), 619–622.

Kostof, S. (1991). *The City Shaped: Urban Patterns and Meanings through History*. London: Thames & Hudson.

Kotkin, J. (2005). *The City: A Global History*. New York: Modern Library.

Kunstler, J. (2011). Back to the future. *Orion*, July/August.

Kusimba, C. (2008). Early African cities: Their role in the shaping of urban and rural interaction spheres. In J. Marcus and J. Sabloff, eds., *The Ancient City: New Perspectives on Urbanism in the Old and New Worlds*. Santa Fe, NM: SAR Press, pp. 229–246.

LaViolette, A. (2008). Swahili cosmopolitanism in Africa and the Indian Ocean world, AD 600–1500. *Archaeologies: Journal of the World Archaeological Congress*, 4(1), 24–49.

LaViolette, A. and Fleisher, J. (2004). The archaeology of sub-Saharan urbanism: Cities and their countrysides. In A. Stahl, ed., *African Archaeology: A Critical Introduction*. Oxford: Blackwell Publishing, pp. 327–352.

LaViolette, A., Fleisher, J., and Horton, M. (2023). Assembling Islamic practice in a Swahili urban landscape, 11th–16th centuries. *Journal of Social Archaeology*, 23(1), 99–124.

Lawler, A. (2008). Boring no more, a trade-savvy Indus emerges. *Science*, 320(5881), 1276–1281.

Lawler, A. (2011). America's lost city. *Science*, 334(6063), 1618–1623.

Leadbetter, M. (2021). The fluid city, urbanism as process. *World Archaeology*, 53(1), 137–157.

Lefebvre, H. (1996). The right to the city. In E. Kofman and E. Lebas, eds., *Writings on Cities*. Oxford: Blackwell, pp. 147–159.

Leick, G. (2001). *Mesopotamia: The Invention of the City*. London: Penguin Books.

Lekson, S. (2018). *A Study of Southwestern Archaeology*. Salt Lake City: University of Utah Press.

Lerner, J. (2014). *Urban Acupuncture*. Washington, DC: Island Press.

Leyser, C., Standen, N., and Wynne-Jones, S. (2018). Settlement, landscape and narrative: What really happened in history. *Past & Present*, 238(Suppl. 13), 232–260.

Lucero, L. (2018). A cosmology of conservation in the ancient Maya world. *Journal of Anthropological Research*, 74(3), 327–359.

Lucero, L., Fletcher, R., and Coningham, R. (2015). From 'collapse' to urban diaspora: The transformation of low-density, dispersed agrarian urbanism. *Antiquity*, 89(347), 1139–1154.

Lucero, L., Gunn, J., and Scarborough, V. (2011). Climate change and Classic Maya water management. *Water*, 3(2), 479–494.

Lynch, K. (1960). *The Image of the City*. Cambridge, MA: MIT Press.

Maaranen, N., Walker, J., and Soltysiak, A. (2022). Societal segmentation and early urbanism in Mesopotamia: Biological distance analysis from Tell Brak using dental morphology. *Journal of Anthropological Archaeology*, 67, p101421.

Magnoni, A., Arden, T., Hutson, S., and Dahlin, B. (2014). The production of space and identity at Classic-period Chunchucmil, Yucatan, Mexico. In A. Creekmore and K. Fisher, eds., *Making Ancient Cities: Space and Place in Early Urban Societies*. Cambridge: Cambridge University Press, pp. 145–180.

Manzanilla, L. (2009). Corporate life in apartment and barrio compounds at Teotihuacan, central Mexico: Craft specialization, hierarchy, and ethnicity. In L. Manzanilla and C. Chapdelaine, eds., *Domestic Life in Prehispanic Capitals: A Study of Specialization, Hierarchy, and Ethnicity*. Memoirs No. 40. Ann Arbor: Museum of Anthropology, University of Michigan, pp. 21–42.

Manzanilla, L. (2015). Cooperation and tensions in multiethnic corporate societies using Teotihuacan, central Mexico, as a case study. *PNAS*, 112(30), 9210–9215.

Manzanilla, L., ed. (2017). *Multiethnicity and Migration at Teopancazco: Investigations of a Teotihuacan Neighborhood Center*. Gainesville: University Press of Florida.

Manzanilla, L. (2018). Corporate societies with exclusionary social components: The Teotihuacan metropolis. *Origini: Prehistory and Protohistory of Ancient Civilizations*, 42, 211–225.

Marcus, J. and Sabloff, J., eds. (2008). *The Ancient City: New Perspectives on Urbanism in the Old and New Worlds*. Santa Fe, NM: SAR Press.

Marken, D. and Arnauld, C., eds. (2023). *Building an Archaeology of Maya Urbanism: Planning and Flexibility in the American Tropics*. Denver: University Press of Colorado.

Mathews, F. (2022). Conservation needs to include a 'story about feeling'. *Biological Conservation*, 272, p109668. https://doi-org.du.idm.oclc.org/ 10.1016/j.biocon.2022.109668.

McAnany, P. and N. Yoffee, eds. (2010). *Questioning Collapse: Human Resilience, Ecological Vulnerability, and the Aftermath of Empire*. New York: Cambridge University Press.

McFarlane, C. (2011). Assemblage and critical urbanism. *City*, 15(2), 204–224.

McGranahan, G., Schensul, D., and Singh, G. (2016). Inclusive urbanization: Can the 2030 agenda be delivered without it? *Environment and Urbanization*, 28(1), 13–34.

McGuirk, J. (2014). *Radical Cities: Across Latin America in Search of a New Architecture*. New York: Verso.

McIntosh, R. (2005). *Ancient Middle Niger: Urbanism and the Self-Organizing Landscape*. Cambridge: Cambridge University Press.

McIntosh, R. and McIntosh, S. (2003). Early urban configurations on the Middle Niger: Clustered cities and landscapes of power. In M. L. Smith, ed., *The Social Construction of Ancient Cities*. Washington, DC: Smithsonian Institution, pp. 103–120.

McIntosh, S. (1997). Urbanism in sub-Saharan Africa. In J. O. Vogel and J. Vogel, eds., *Encyclopedia of Precolonial Africa*. Walnut Creek, CA: Altamira, pp. 461–465.

McLaren, D. and Agyeman. J. (2015). *Sharing Cities: A Case for Truly Smart and Sustainable Cities.* Cambridge, MA: MIT Press.

McMahon, A. (2013a). Mesopotamia. In P. Clark, ed., *The Oxford Handbook of Cities in World History*. Oxford: Oxford University Press, pp. 31–48.

McMahon, A. (2013b). Space, sound, and light: Toward a sensory experience of ancient monumental architecture. *American Journal of Archaeology*, 117(2), 163–179.

McMahon, A. (2014). Urbanism and the prehistory of violent conflict: Tell Brak, northeast Syria. ArchéOrient – Le Blog [online]. https://archeorient .hypotheses.org/2797.

McMahon, A., Pittman, H., Al-Rawi, Z. et al. (2023). Dense urbanism and economic multi-centrism at third-millennium BC Lagash. *Antiquity*, 97(393), 596–615.

McMillan, B. (2022). Urban narratives and urban history: On presentation and interpretation. *Journal of Urban History*, 49(4), 929–935.

Meddeb, R. and Handforth, C. (2022). We need smarter cities, not 'smart cities'. *MIT Technology Review*, 125(4), 16–17.

Mehaffy, M. (2018). Five takeaways from the 2018 world urban forum. *Public Square*, March 19 [online]. www.cnu.org/publicsquare/2018/03/19/five-take aways-2018-world-urban-forum.

Mehaffy, M. (2019). We need 'Goldilocks', not 'voodoo' urbanism. *Public Square*, January 16 [online]. www.cnu.org/publicsquare/2019/01/16/we-need-'goldilocks'-not-'voodoo'-urbanism.

Mehaffy, M. and Haas, T. (2018). Informality in the new urban agenda: A 'new paradigm'? *Berkeley Planning Journal*, 30(1), 6–22.

Mellaart, J. (1967). *Çatal Hüyük: A Neolithic Town in Anatolia*. New York: McGraw Hill.

Merrifield, A. (2014). *The New Urban Question*. London: Pluto Press.

Middleton, G. (2017). The show must go on: Collapse, resilience, and transformation in 21st-century archaeology. *Reviews in Anthropology*, 46(2–3), 78–105.

Millhauser, J. and Earle, T. (2022). Biodiversity and the human past: Lessons for conservation biology. *Biological Conservation*, 272, p.109599. https://doi-org.du.idm.oclc.org/10.1016/j.biocon.2022.109599.

Mills, B. (2023). From frontier to centre place: The dynamic trajectory of the Chaco world. *Journal of Urban Archaeology*, 7, 215–252.

Mixter, D. (2019). Community resilience and urban planning during the ninth-century Maya collapse: A case study from Actuncan, Belize. *Cambridge Archaeological Journal*, 30(2), 219–237.

Mosher, M. (2017). The architecture of Mohenjo-Daro as evidence for the organization of Indus civilization neighbourhoods. PhD dissertation, University of Toronto.

Müller, Rassmann, J. K. and Videiko, M. (2016). *Trypillia Mega-Sites and European Prehistory 4100–3400 BCE*. Abingdon: Routledge.

Murphy, J. and Crumley, C. (2022). *If the Past Teaches, What Does the Future Learn? Ancient Urban Regions and the Durable Future*. Delft: TU Delft.

Murtha, T. (2023). The living landscape: Livelihoods and opportunities in the city and region of ancient Tikal. In D. Marken and M. Arnauld, eds., *Building an Archaeology of Maya Urbanism: Planning and Flexibility in the American Tropics*. Denver: University Press of Colorado, pp. 315–348.

Myers, G. (2011). Why Africa's cities matter. *African Geographical Review*, 30(1), 101–106.

Newitz, A. (2021). *Four Lost Cities: A Secret History of the Urban Age*. New York: W. W. Norton and Company.

Nichols, D. (2016). Teotihuacan. *Journal of Archaeological Research*, 24(1), 1–74.

Noble, G. (2013). Cosmopolitan habits: The capacities and habitats of intercultural conviviality. *Body and Society*, 19(2–3), 162–185.

Norwood, A. and Smith, M. E. (2022). Urban open space and governance in ancient Mesoamerica. *Journal of Archaeological Method and Theory*, 29(3), 939–961.

Novak, M. (2004). From Ashur to Nineveh: The Assyrian town-planning programme. *Papers of the XLIXe Rencontre Assyriologique Internationale*, 1 (Iraq 66), 177–185.

O'Brien, C. (2023). Empty office buildings are being turned into vertical farms. *Smithsonian Magazine*, July 11. www.smithsonianmag.com/innovation/empty-office-buildings-are-being-turned-into-vertical-farms-180982502/.

Ohlrau, R. (2022). Trypillia mega-sites: Neither urban nor low-density? *Journal of Urban Archaeology* 5, 81–100.

Ortiz, C. (2023). Storytelling otherwise: Decolonising storytelling in planning. *Planning Theory*, 22(2), 177–200.

Ortman, S. (2019). A new kind of relevance for archaeology. *Frontiers in Digital Humanities*, 6, p16. https://doi.org/10.3389/fdigh.2019.00016.

Ortman, S., Cabaniss, A., Sturm, J., and Bettencourt, L. (2015). Settlement scaling and increasing returns in an ancient society. *Science Advances*, 1(1), p.e1400066. https://doi.org/10.1126/sciadv.1400066.

Ortman, S., Lobo, J., and Smith, M. E. (2020). Cities: Complexity, theory and history. *PLoS ONE*, 15(12), p.e0243621. https://doi.org/10.1371/journal.pone.0243621.

Ortman, S., Smith, M. E., Lobo, J., and Bettencourt, L. (2020). Why archaeology is necessary for a theory of urbanization. *Journal of Urban Archaeology*, 1, 152–167.

Otto, A. (2015). Neo-Assyrian capital cities: From imperial headquarters to cosmopolitan cities. In N. Yoffee, ed., *Early Cities in Comparative Perspective: 4000 BCE–1200 CE*. Cambridge: Cambridge University Press, pp. 469–490.

Patel, S. (2014). Stone towns of the Swahili coast. *Archaeology*, 61(1), January/February, pp. 42–49.

Pauketat, T. (2019). Fragile Cahokian and Chacoan orders and infrastructures. In N. Yoffee, ed., *The Evolution of Fragility: Setting the Terms*. Cambridge: McDonald Institute for Archaeological Research, pp. 89–108.

Pauketat, T. (2020a). Introducing new materialisms, rethinking ancient urbanisms. In S. Alt and T. Pauketat, eds. *New Materialisms Ancient Urbanisms*. London: Routledge, pp. 1–18.

Pauketat, T. (2020b). What constituted Cahokian urbanism? In G. Farhat, ed., *Landscapes of Preindustrial Urbanism*. Washington, DC: Dumbarton Oaks, pp. 89–111.

Pauketat, T. and Alt, S., eds. (2015). *Medieval Mississippians: The Cahokian World*. Santa Fe, NM: SAR Press.

Pauketat, T., Alt, S., Betzenhauser, A., Kruchten, J., and Benson, E. (2023). Cahokia as urban anomaly. *Journal of Urban Archaeology*, 7, 253–274.

Pauketat, T., Alt, S. and Kruchten, J. (2015). City of earth and wood: New Cahokia and its material-historical implications. In N. Yoffee, ed., *Early Cities in Comparative Perspective: 4000 BCE–1200 CE*. Cambridge: Cambridge University Press, pp. 437–454.

Pawlowicz, M., Fleisher, J., and Wynne-Jones, S. (2021). Exploring Swahili urbanism through survey of Songo Mnara Island, Tanzania. *The Journal of*

Island and Coastal Archaeology. https://doi.org/10.1080/15564894.2021 .1988007.

Peattie, L. (1994). An argument for slums. *Journal of Planning Education and Research*, 13(2), 136–142.

Peregrine, P., S, Ortman, and E. Rupley (2014). Social complexity at Cahokia. Santa Fe Institute Working Paper No. 2014-03-004 [online]. www.santafe .edu/research/results/working-papers/social-complexity-at-cahokia.

Petrie, C. (2013). South Asia. In P. Clark, ed., *The Oxford Handbook of Cities in World History.* Oxford: Oxford University Press, pp. 83–104.

Petrie, C. (2017). Looking beneath the veneer: Thoughts about environmental and cultural diversity in the Indus civilization. In D. Frenez, G. Jamison, R. Law, M. Vidale, and R. Meadow, eds., *Walking with the Unicorn: Social Organization and Material Culture in Ancient South Asia.* Oxford: Archaeopress Publishing, pp. 453–474.

Petrie, C. (2019). Diversity, variability, adaptation, and 'fragility' in the Indus civilization. In N. Yoffee, ed., *The Evolution of Fragility: Setting the Terms.* Cambridge: McDonald Institute for Archaeological Research, pp. 109–133.

Pollard, E., Fleisher, J., and Wynne-Jones, S. (2012). Beyond the stone town: Maritime architecture at fourteenth-fifteenth century Songo Mnara, Tanzania. *Journal of Maritime Archaeology*, 7(1), 43–62.

Pool, C. and Loughlin, M. (2016). Tres Zapotes: The evolution of a resilient polity in the Olmec heartland of Mexico. In R. Faulseit, ed., *Beyond Collapse: Archaeological Perspectives on Resilience, Revitalization, and Transformation in Complex Societies.* Carbondale, IL: Center for Archaeological Investigations, pp 287–309.

Pool, C. and Loughlin, M. (2017). Creating memory and negotiating power in the Olmec heartland. *Journal of Archaeological Method and Theory*, 24(1), 229–260.

Pool, C. and Loughlin, M. (2022). Early urbanization in the Formative Gulf Lowlands, Mexico. In M. Love and J. Guernsey, eds., *Early Mesoamerican Cities: Urbanism and Urbanization in the Formative Period.* Cambridge: Cambridge University Press, pp. 50–72.

Porter, L. (2011). Informality, the commons and the paradoxes for planning: Debates for informality and planning. *Planning Theory and Practice*, 12(1), 115–153.

Prümers, H., Betancourt, C., Iriarte, J., Robinson, M., and Schaich. (2022). Lidar reveals pre-Hispanic low-density urbanism in the Bolivian Amazon. *Nature*, 606, 325–328. https://doi.org/10.1038/s41586-022-04780-4.

Pugh, T., Rice, P., Chan Nieto, E., and Georges, J. (2022a). Complexity, cooperation, and public goods: Quality of place at Nixtun-Ch'ich', Petén,

Guatemala. *Frontiers in Political Science*, 4, p.805888. https://doi.org/10.3389/fpos.2022.805888.

Pugh, T., Rice, P., Nieto, E., Meranda, M., and Milley, D. (2022b). Middle Preclassic hydraulic planning at Nixtun-Ch'ich', Peten, Guatemala. *Ancient Mesoamerica*, 33(3), 589–603.

Raja, R. and Sindbæk, S. (2022). Anomalocivitas – editorial. *Journal of Urban Archaeology*, 5, 13–18.

Raja, R. and Sindbæk, S. (2023). David and Goliath: Giants and dwarfs in settlement archaeology – editorial. *Journal of Urban Archaeology*, 7, 15–16.

Ramzy, N. (2016). Morphological logic in historical settlements: Space syntax analyses of residential districts at Mohenjo-Daro, Kahun and Ur. *Urban Design International*, 21(1), 41–54.

Robbins Schug, G. (2020). Ritual, urbanism, and the everyday: Mortuary behavior in the Indus civilization. In T. Betsinger and S. DeWitte, eds., *The Bioarchaeology of Urbanization: The Biological, Demographic, and Social Consequences of Living in Cities*. Cham: Springer International, pp. 49–72.

Robertshaw, P. (2019). Fragile states in sub-Saharan Africa. In N. Yoffee, ed., *The Evolution of Fragility: Setting the Terms*. Cambridge: McDonald Institute for Archaeological Research, pp. 135–159.

Robertson, I. (2008). *Insubstantial Residential Structures at Teotihuacan, Mexico*. Report. Coral Gables, FL: FAMSI [online]. www.famsi.org/reports/06103/06103Robertson01.pdf.

Robinson, J. (2006). *Ordinary Cities: Between Modernity and Development*. London: Routledge.

Rødland, H., Wynne-Jones, S., Wood, M., and Fleisher, J. (2020). No such thing as invisible people: Toward an archaeology of slavery at the fifteenth-century Swahili site of Songo Mnara. *Azania: Archaeological Research in Africa*, 55(4), 439–457.

Rojas, A. and Dávila, N. B. (2020). Studying ancient water management in Monte Albán, Mexico, to solve water issues, improve urban living, and protect heritage in the present. In C. Hein, ed., *Adaptive Strategies for Water Heritage: Past, Present, and Future*. Cham: Springer, pp. 59–77.

Rose, J. (2016). *The Well-Tempered City: What Modern Science, Ancient Civilizations, and Human Nature Teach Us about the Future of Urban Life*. New York: HarperCollins Publishers.

Roy, A. (2009). The 21st-century metropolis: New geographies of theory. *Regional Studies* 43(6), 819–830.

Sabloff, J. (2008). *Archaeology Matters: Action Archaeology in The Modern World*. London: Routledge.

Saitta, D. (2020). *Intercultural Urbanism: City Planning from the Ancient World to the Modern Day*. London: Bloomsbury.

Sampson, R. (2017). Urban sustainability in an age of enduring inequalities: Advancing theory and econometrics for the 21st century city. *PNAS*, 114(34), 8957–8962.

Sandercock, L. (1998). *Towards Cosmopolis: Planning for Multicultural Cities*. Chichester: John Wiley & Sons.

Sandercock, L. (2003). *Cosmopolis II: Mongrel Cities in the 21st Century*. London: Continuum.

Sandoval-Strausz, A. (2019). *Barrio America: How Latino Immigrants Saved the American City*. New York: Basic Books.

Scarborough, V. and Isendahl, C. (2020). Distributed urban network systems in the tropical archaeological record: Toward a model for urban sustainability in the era of climate change. *The Anthropocene Review*, 7(3), 208–230.

Scarborough, V. and Lucero, L. (2010). The non-hierarchical development of complexity in the semi-tropics: Water and cooperation. *Water History*, 2, 185–205.

Schillaci, M. (2003). The development of population diversity at Chaco Canyon. *Kiva*, 68(3), 221–245.

Schwenkel, C. (2022). What is critical – and anthropological – about critical urban anthropology? *City and Society*, 34(1), 47–50.

Sennett, R. (2013). Reflections on the public realm. In G. Bridge and S. Watson, eds., *The New Blackwell Companion to the City*. London: Blackwell, pp. 390–397.

Sennett, R. (2018). *Building and Dwelling: Ethics for the City*. New York: Farrar, Straus and Giroux.

Simon, D. and Adam-Bradford, A. (2016). Archaeology and contemporary dynamics for more sustainable, resilient cities in the peri-urban interface. In B. Maheshwari, V. Singh, and B. Thoradeniya, eds, *Balanced Urban Development: Options and Strategies for Liveable Cities*. Cham: Springer, pp. 57–83.

Sindbæk, S. (2022). Weak ties and strange attractors: Anomalocivitas and the archaeology of urban origins. *Journal of Urban Archaeology*, 5, 19–32.

Sjoberg, G. (1960). *The Preindustrial City: Past and Present*. New York: The Free Press.

Smith, A. (2003). *The Political Landscape: Constellations of Authority in Early Complex Polities*. Berkeley: University of California Press.

Smith, M. E. (2009). Just how comparative is comparative urban geography? A perspective from archaeology. *Urban Geography*, 30(2), 113–117.

Smith, M. E. (2011). Empirical urban theory for archaeologists. *Journal of Archaeological Method and Theory*, 18(3), 167–192.

Smith, M. E. (2017). The Teotihuacan anomaly: The historical trajectory of urban design in ancient Central Mexico. *Open Archaeology*, 3(1), 175–193.

Smith, M. E. (2019). Quality of life and prosperity in ancient households and communities. In C. Isendahl and D. Stump, eds., *The Oxford Handbook of Historical Ecology and Applied Archaeology*. Oxford: Oxford University Press, pp. 486–505.

Smith, M. E. (2021). Why archaeology's relevance to global challenges has not been recognized. *Antiquity*, 95(382), 1061–1069.

Smith, M. E. (2023a). *Urban Life in The Distant Past: The Prehistory of Energized Crowding*. Cambridge: Cambridge University Press.

Smith, M. E. (2023b). How can research on past urban adaptations be made useful for sustainability science? *Global Sustainability*, 6, e4. https://doi.org/10.1017/sus.2023.2.

Smith, M. E. (2023c). Urban success and urban adaptation over the long run. *Open Archaeology*, 9(1), p.20220285. https://doi.org/10.1515/opar-2022-0285.

Smith, M. E., Chatterjee, A., Huster, A. C., Stewart, S., and Forest, M. (2019). Apartment compounds, households, and population in the ancient city of Teotihuacan, Mexico. *Ancient Mesoamerica*, 30(3), 399–418.

Smith, M. E., Engquist, A., Carvajal, C. et al. (2015). Neighborhood formation in semi-urban settlements. *Journal of Urbanism*, 8(2), 173–198.

Smith, M. E., Lobo, J., Peeples, M. et al. (2021). The persistence of ancient settlements and urban sustainability. *PNAS*, 118(20), p.e2018155118. https://doi.org/10.1073/pnas.2018155118.

Smith, M. E., Ortman, S., and Lobo, J. (2023). Heritage sites, climate change, and urban science. *Urban Climate*, 47, p.101371. https://doi.org/10.1016/j.uclim.2022.101371.

Smith, M. E., Ur, J., and Feinman, G. (2014). Jane Jacobs' 'Cities First' model and archaeological reality. *International Journal of Urban and Regional Research*, 38(4), 1525–1535.

Smith, M. L., ed. (2003a). *The Social Construction of Ancient Cities*. Washington, DC: Smithsonian Institution.

Smith, M. L. (2003b). Introduction. In M. L. Smith, ed., *The Social Construction of Ancient Cities*. Washington, DC: Smithsonian Institution, pp. 1–36.

Smith, M. L. (2006). The archaeology of South Asian cities. *Journal of Archaeological Research*, 14(2), 97–142.

Smith, M. L. (2008). Urban empty spaces: Contentious places for consensus-building. *Archaeological Dialogues*, 15(2), 216–231.

Smith, M. L. (2019). *Cities: The First 6,000 Years*. New York: Viking.

Soja, E. (2018). Accentuate the regional. In T. Haas and H. Westlund, eds., *In the Post-Urban World: Emergent Transformation of Cities and Regions in the Innovative Global Economy*. London: Routledge, pp. 197–209.

Solis, R. (2006). America's first city? The case of Late Archaic Caral. In W. Isbell and H. Silverman, eds., *Andean Archaeology III: North and South*. Boston, MA: Springer, pp. 28–66.

Spence, M., White, C., Rattray, E., and Longstaffe, F. (2005). Past lives in different places: The origins and relationships of Teotihuacan's foreign residents. In R. Blanton, ed., *Settlement, Subsistence, and Social Complexity: Essays Honoring the Legacy of Jeffrey R. Parsons*. Los Angeles, CA: Cotsen Institute of Archaeology Press, pp. 155–197.

Stahl, A. (2020). Assembling 'effective archaeologies' toward equitable futures. *American Anthropologist*, 122(1), 37–50.

Stanley, B., Dennehy, T., Smith, M. E. et al. (2016). Service access in premodern cities: An exploratory comparison of spatial equity. *Journal of Urban History*, 42(1), 121–144.

Stanton, T., Taube, K., León, J. et al. (2023). Urbanizing paradise: The implications of pervasive images of Flower World across Chichen Itza. In D. Marken and M. Arnauld, eds., *Building an Archaeology of Maya Urbanism: Planning and Flexibility in the American Tropics*. Denver: University Press of Colorado, pp. 148–174.

Stark, B. (2014). Urban gardens and parks in pre-modern states and empires. *Cambridge Archaeological Journal*, 24(1), 87–115.

Stark, B. and Stoner, W. (2022). Mixed governance principles in the Gulf Lowlands of Mesoamerica. *Frontiers in Political Science*, 4, p.814545. https://doi.org/10.3389/fpos.2022.814545.

Stauffer, J., Grooms, S., Hu, L. et al. (2023). Reimagining the development of downtown Cahokia using remote sensing visualizations from the western edge of the Grand Plaza. *Land*, 12(2), 342–367.

Steyn, G. (2007). Types and typologies of African urbanism. *South African Journal of Art History*, 22(2), 49–65.

Stoner, W. and Stark, B. (2022). Distributed urban networks in the Gulf Lowlands of Veracruz. *Journal of Archaeological Research*, 31(3), 449–501. https://doi.org/10.1007/s10814-022-09178-4.

Storey, G., ed. (2006). *Urbanism in the Preindustrial World: Cross-Cultural Approaches*. Tuscaloosa: University of Alabama Press.

Storey, G. (2020). *The Archaeology of Ancient Cities*. Clinton Corners, NY: Eliot Erner Publications.

Stuart, D. (2000). *Anasazi America*. Albuquerque: University of New Mexico Press.

Stuart, D. (2006). The Chaco Ancestral Puebloans: Lessons learned. In V. Price and B. Morrow, eds., *Canyon Gardens: The Ancient Pueblo Landscapes of the American Southwest*. Albuquerque: University of New Mexico Press, pp. 189–203.

Sugiyama, S. (2022). The nature of early urbanism at Teotihuacan. In M. Love and J. Guernsey, eds., *Early Mesoamerican Cities: Urbanism and Urbanization in the Formative Period*. Cambridge: Cambridge University Press, pp. 170–198.

Sussman, A. and Hollander, J. (2015). *Cognitive Architecture: Designing for How We Respond to the Built Environment*. New York: Routledge.

Tainter, J. (2019). Cahokia: Urbanization, metabolism, and collapse. *Frontiers in Sustainable Cities*, 1, 6. https://doi.org/10.3389/frsc.2019.00006.

Taylor, P. (2012). Extraordinary cities: Early 'city-ness' and the origins of agriculture and states. *International Journal of Urban and Regional Research*, 36(3), 415–447.

Taylor, P. (2019). City generics: External urban relations in ancient-Mesopotamian and modern-global city networks. *Urban Geography*, 40(8), 1210–1230.

Thomason, A. (2016). The sense-scapes of Neo-Assyrian capital cities: Royal authority and bodily experience. *Cambridge Archaeological Journal*, 26(2), 243–264.

Throgmorton, J. (2003). Planning as persuasive storytelling in a global-scale web of relationships. *Planning Theory*, 2(2), 125–151.

Tilly, C. (1996). What good is urban history? *Journal of Urban History* 22(6), 702–719.

United Nations (2017). *The New Urban Agenda*. New York: United Nations.

Ur, J. (2013). The morphology of Neo-Assyrian cities. *Subartu*, 6–7, 11–22.

Ur, J. (2014). Households and the emergence of cities in ancient Mesopotamia. *Cambridge Archaeological Journal*, 24(2), 249–268.

Ur, J. (2016). The birth of cities in ancient West Asia. In A. Tsuneki, ed., *Ancient West Asian Civilization: Geoenvironment and Society in the Pre-Islamic Middle East*. Singapore: Springer, pp. 133–147.

Ur, J. (2020). Space and structure in early Mesopotamian cities. In G. Farhat, ed., *Landscapes of Preindustrial Urbanism*. Washington, DC: Dumbarton Oaks, pp. 37–59.

Valentine, B., Kamenov, G., Kenoyer, J. et al. (2015). Evidence for patterns of selective urban migration in the Greater Indus Valley (2600–1900 BC): A lead and strontium isotope mortuary analysis. *PLoS ONE*, 10(4), p.e0123103. https://doi.org/10.1371/journal.pone.0123103.

Van De Mieroop, M. (1997). *The Ancient Mesopotamian City*. Oxford: Clarendon Press.

Van De Mieroop, M. (2003). Reading Babylon. *American Journal of Archaeology*, 107(2), 257–275.

Vidale, M. (2010). Aspects of palace life at Mohenjo-Daro. *South Asian Studies*, 26(1), 59–76.

Wade, L. (2017a). Kings of cooperation. *Archaeology*, 70(2), March/April, pp. 27–29.

Wade, L. (2017b). Unearthing democracy's roots. *Science*, 355(6330), 1114–1118.

Walker, J. (2023). The death and life of agricultural cities. In D. Marken and M. Arnauld, eds., *Building an Archaeology of Maya Urbanism: Planning and Flexibility in the American Tropics*. Denver: University Press of Colorado, pp. 437–459.

Wengrow, D. (2018). The origins of civic life – a global perspective. *Origini: The Prehistory and Protohistory of Ancient Civilizations*, 42, 25–44.

Werbner, P. (2014). Cosmopolitanism: Cosmopolitan cities and the dialectics of living together with difference. In D. Nonini, ed., *A Companion to Urban Anthropology*. Chichester: John Wiley and Sons, pp. 306–326.

West, A. (2011). It's biology: All cities are alike. *Sydney Morning Herald*, July 23 [online]. www.smh.com.au/national/its-biology-all-cities-are-alike-20110722-1hsue.html

West, G. (2018). *Scale: The Universal Laws of Life, Growth, and Death in Organisms, Cities, and Companies*. New York: Penguin.

Wills, W. (2009). Cultural identity and the archaeological construction of historical narratives: An example from Chaco Canyon. *Journal of Archaeological Method and Theory*, 16(4), 283–319.

Wilson, B. (2020). *Metropolis: A History of Humankind's Greatest Invention*. London: Jonathan Cape.

Wilson, J. (1960). Egypt through the New Kingdom: Civilization without cities. In C. Kraeling and R. McAdams, eds., *City Invincible: A Symposium on Urbanization and Cultural Development in the Ancient Near East*. Chicago, IL: University of Chicago Press, pp. 124–164.

Wood, P. and C. Landry (2008). *The Intercultural City: Planning for Diversity Advantage*. London: Earthscan.

Woolf, G. (2020). *The Life and Death of Ancient Cities: A Natural History*. Oxford: Oxford University Press.

Wright, R. (2010). *The Ancient Indus: Urbanism, Economy, and Society*. Cambridge: Cambridge University Press.

Wynne-Jones, S. (2018). The social composition of Swahili society. In S. Wynne-Jones and A. LaViolette, eds., *The Swahili World*. London: Routledge, pp. 293–205.

Wynne-Jones, S. and Fleisher, J. (2015). Fifty years in the archaeology of the eastern African coast: A methodological history. *Azania: Archaeological Research in Africa*, 50(4), 519–541.

Wynne-Jones, S. and Fleisher, J. (2016). The multiple territories of Swahili urban landscapes. *World Archaeology*, 48(3), 349–362.

Yeung, P. (2023). Can a city feed itself? *Bloomberg News*, July 6. www.bloom berg.com/news/features/2023-07-07/in-quest-for-food-security-cities-test-limits-of-urban-agriculture.

Yoffee, N. (2005). *Myths of the Archaic State*. Cambridge: Cambridge University Press.

Yoffee, N. (2009). Making ancient cities plausible. *Reviews in Anthropology*, 38(4), 264–289.

Yoffee, N., ed. (2015). *Early Cities in Comparative Perspective, 4000 BCE–1200 CE*. Cambridge: Cambridge University Press.

Yoffee, N. (2016). The power of infrastructures: A counternarrative and a speculation. *Journal of Archaeological Method and Theory*, 23(4), 1053–1065.

Yoffee, N. (2022). Experimental cities? In M. Love and J. Guernsey, eds., *Early Mesoamerican Cities: Urbanism and Urbanization in the Formative Period*. Cambridge: Cambridge University Press, pp. 238–246.

Yoffee, N. and Seri, A. (2019). Negotiating fragility in ancient Mesopotamia: Arenas of contestation and institutions of resistance. In N. Yoffee, ed., *The Evolution of Fragility: Setting the Terms*. Cambridge: McDonald Institute for Archaeological Research, pp. 183–196.

York, A., Smith, M. E., Stanley, B. et al. (2011). Ethnic and class clustering through the ages: A transdisciplinary approach to urban neighborhood social patterns. *Urban Studies*, 48(11), 2399–2415.

Zeiderman, A. and Dawson, K. (2022). Urban futures: Idealization, capitalization, securitization. *City*, 26(2–3), 261–280.

Anthropological Archaeology in the 21st Century

Eli Dollarhide

New York University Abu Dhabi

Eli Dollarhide is an archaeological anthropologist who specializes in the prehistory of the Middle East, with a focus on the Persian Gulf. His research investigates the role of small and rural settlements in the development of Bronze Age exchange networks and political systems. Dollarhide codirects research at the UNESCO World Heritage Site of Bat, Oman and investigates ancient ceramic technologies. See https://nyuad.nyu.edu/en/research/faculty-labs-and-projects/humanities-research-fellowship-program/research-fellows/eli-dollarhide.html.

Michael Galaty

University of Michigan

Michael Galaty is Professor of Anthropology in the Department of Anthropology and Director and Curator of European and Mediterranean Archaeology in the Museum of Anthropological Archaeology at the University of Michigan. He conducts fieldwork in Albania, Greece, and Kosovo, with a focus on the prehistoric origins of social inequalities. To that end, he utilizes intensive regional survey and targeted excavations, along with various laboratory techniques, to track the changing economic and political factors that lead to transformative changes in Mediterranean and Balkan social systems, during the Bronze Age, in particular.

Junko Habu

University of California, Berkeley

Junko Habu is Professor of Anthropology and Chair of the Center for Japanese Studies, University of California – Berkeley, and Affiliate Professor of the Research Institute for Humanity and Nature. She has published extensively on Japanese and East Asian archaeology, hunter-gatherer archaeology, and historical ecology. Her current research focuses on the intersection of archaeology, agroecology, and traditional ecological knowledge to consider the resilience of socioeconomic systems in the past, present, and future. For more information, see https://junkohabu.com/.

Patricia A. McAnany

University of North Carolina at Chapel Hill

Patricia A. McAnany, Kenan Eminent Professor and Chair of Anthropology at the University of North Carolina at Chapel Hill (UNC), is a codirector of Proyecto Arqueológico Colaborativo del Oriente de Yucatán – a community-archaeology project at Tahcabo, Yucatán, México. She cofounded and directs InHerit: Indigenous Heritage Passed to Present (www.in-herit.org), a UNC program that generates collaborative research and education projects focused on archaeology and cultural heritage with communities in the Maya region and North Carolina. She is the author of several books (most recently *Maya Cultural Heritage: How Archaeologists and Indigenous Peoples Engage the Past*) as well as journal articles and book chapters on a range of archaeological and heritage topics.

John K. Millhauser
North Carolina State University

John K. Millhauser is Associate Professor of Anthropology in the Department of Sociology and Anthropology at North Carolina State University. His archaeological work in Mexico centers on rural communities and social economies under Mexica and Spanish rule. His current research integrates economic anthropology and political ecology to better understand the origins of poverty and structural violence. For more information, see chass.ncsu.edu/people/jkmillha/.

Rita Wright
New York University

Rita Wright is Professor Emerita of Anthropology at New York University. Using Near Eastern texts as secondary sources and ancient technologies (ceramics and weaving), she investigates divisions of labor and women's contributions to history. In the field, she has conducted research in Afghanistan, Pakistan, and Iran, predominately in Baluchistan at Mehrgarh and the Punjab, Pakistan, at the city of Harappa. Her Landscape and Settlement survey of Harappa's rural areas is the first conducted in studies of the Indus civilization. She is the founder and editor of the Cambridge University Press Case Studies in Early Societies series, especially *The Ancient Indus: Urbanism, Economy, and Society* (2010).

About the Series

This series offers anthropological and contemporary perspectives in the study of prehistoric and historic societies globally and cutting-edge research with balanced coverage of well-known sites and understudied times and places. We solicit contributions based on three themes: (1) new methods and technologies producing fresh understandings of the past; (2) theoretical approaches challenging basic concepts and offering new insights; (3) archaeological responses for the 21st century providing informed choices for the present. Individual Elements focus on specific sites and regions that highlight the diversity of human experience around the world and across history, which include scholars working throughout North America, Mesoamerica, Europe and the Mediterranean, Africa, the Middle East, and South and East Asia and readers with an avid interest in the latest frontiers in archaeological thought. The media-rich Elements will be an important resource for students, scholars.

Cambridge Elements $\equiv$

Anthropological Archaeology in the 21st Century

Elements in the Series

Printed in the United States
by Baker & Taylor Publisher Services